Backcountry Snowboarding
and Skiing in the
Northern Sierra

George Hurchalla

SPOT X Guides

Stuart, FL

Please feel free to offer corrections, improvements, wisecracks, and your own experiences to help make this guide as up to date, useful, and entertaining as possible, via mail at:

Spot X Images
5775 SE Nassau Ter   or email: info@spotximages.com
Stuart, FL 34997

Cover and Text Design: George Hurchalla
Photo Credits: All photos are   by George Hurchalla except where noted.
Maps by George Hurchalla

Library of Congress Data

ISBN 0-9747335-0-4
Library of Congress Control Number: 2003098680

Printed in Hong Kong
First Edition/First Printing

Contents

cover photo: Erik Wilhelm
              Babycham Couloir, Mt Tallac

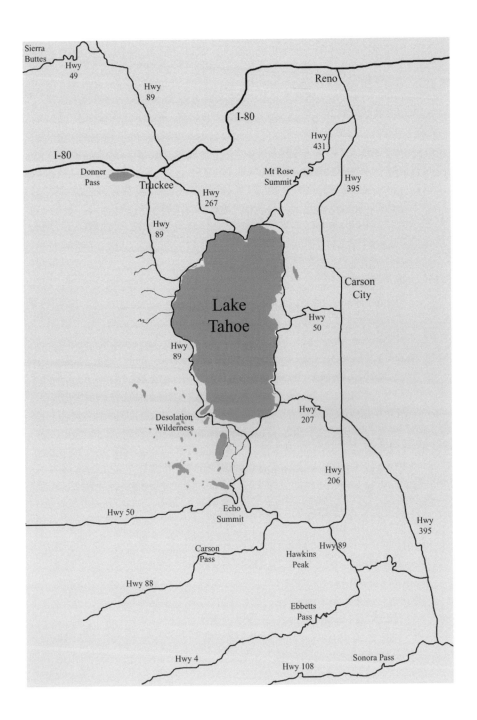

Acknowledgements

There are some people I'd like to thank for making my backcountry experience as rich as it has been:

Mark Kircher and Tom Anderson at Alpenglow in Tahoe City, who spent hours giving me feedback on my ideas, and making sure I respected those who had come before me. Dave Frissyn, who has been a solid backcountry partner from one end of the range to the other. Erik Wilhelm, who was always ready to step up and go big - Babycham, Aloha, Sonora, and all the other epic adventures. Liz McMillan, for being a cool housemate and one of the most solid backcountry gals I ever had the pleasure of riding with. Peter Underwood, who has always had a good word and a smile since I first arrived in Tahoe. Jim Galletto, for the Yogurt Factory coffee, and for being the hardest of the hardcore without ever talking about it. And Grant Barta, for his photos and knowledge.

This book is in memory of Aaron Martin (1971-2002, RIP), a great friend and backcountry mountaineer inspiration, who introduced me to Mt Tallac. I would recommend anyone to search for a copy of the out-of-print book *The Ski Bum*, by French author Romain Gary, which Aaron often proclaimed as his favorite book. It is undoubtedly the greatest piece of literature ever written about skiing. I thought of Aaron often when I first read it, the escape artist in him, and his love of the freedom of skiing the big lines of Chamonix and Le Grave. The protagonist Lenny was so very like Aaron.

"People always liked him, he had the kind of blond good looks that made every woman feel protective or worse, and as there was no language barrier there was little you could do about it...Everything is always much easier when you don't speak the language. You don't have to be rude to people. You don't have to tell them: No thanks, I don't want to go and stay with you in Miami, I have no use for anything that lies below six thousand feet, and that includes you. None of the bums cared a damn what they did when there was no snow...It simply didn't matter to a bum what he did below six thousand feet. The only thing that mattered was not to get trapped in the glue down there..."

"Lenny often wondered why so many ski bums were Americans, maybe because when you have a really big country behind you, you have got to run. You just don't want the responsibility. And it was a nice, comfortable thing to be a young American abroad, because you had the reputation of being dumb and inarticulate anyway, and what with the language barrier you were really safe there. All you had to do was to conform to their idea of the young, innocent American in Europe, and to turn on that typically American grin, standing in some street with your sleeping bag and your skis, and looking nice, handsome, and lost, and even though the police knew you were a vagrant they would leave you alone. America could still do a lot of things for you, provided you left it far behind you...And the nice thing about Europe is that they all have the American Dream over here. They all know for sure that even though you are arrested for sleeping in public places, railway stations or under a bridge, you're not a bum, without a franc in your pocket and no change of clothes, they think you're only a little crazy and looking for experience, they know you'll be back next year driving a Cadillac."

Aaron Martin

Preface

Guide books, by their nature, are bound to be a bit controversial. They are probably even more so when they are covering ground that a lot of different people have a stake in. For awhile there have been heated discussions about overcrowding in certain parts of the backcountry around Tahoe. Many locals jealously guard their secret places, and my wanton dispensation of information concerning these spots may not be taken well. The fact is, there are few actual secrets to give away in Northern Sierra backcountry; it's all a matter of how much commitment you have to getting to it.

There is a belief I find among backcountry enthusiasts that no one has the right to go to a place they haven't found on their own, and that I am making it too easy. Possibly. At the same time, some hikers may not feel I provide enough specific access information throughout the guide. I try to strike a balance to make sure the reader knows where to go while not getting carried away with instructions, so that a sense of adventure and discovery is still there. I feel that the backcountry of the Northern Sierra is so vast that there is room for a few more of us. Where there isn't enough room is in some of the parking areas for these places, and if I don't provide specific directions about where to start from, it may be because the parking is quasi-legal. In other cases it's because there are so many different possibilities that I leave it to the reader to choose their best line of approach. The fluid nature of access in the Tahoe Basin is one of the many ways population causes a difference in comparison to the cut-and-dried access of the mountain passes and the wild mountains to the south.

I snowboard and I used to work as a photographer and writer in the snowboard industry, so much of the emphasis on snowboarding in here reflects that. The old rivalries between skiing and snowboarding are a thing of the past, though, and there's little difference between the terrain that captures the interest of skiers and snowboarders. New school skiers are building kickers and quarterpipes in the backcountry, and snowboarders are riding the steepest of chutes. This book delves deeper than most backcountry guides do into steep, challenging terrain available, but reading this doesn't make your skills any better. Sooner or later, the backcountry opens up an extra large can of whup ass on those who don't approach it cautiously.

Because snowboarders have traditionally had the most difficulty accessing backcountry terrain due to the slowness of post-holing along in their boots, for some time they were thought of as an almost un-natural addition to the backcountry. What gets forgotten, even by snowboarders themselves, is that backcountry is where snowboarding originated. For over a decade, snow-boarders hiked exclusively up hills and gullies and peaks because ski resorts wouldn't allow them. There's nothing more natural than snowboarders in the backcountry, and with the advent of ultralight snowshoes and split boards, snowboarders are able to keep pace with everyone else now.

As far as snowmobiles in the backcountry, which many snowboarders and skiers are using with increasing frequency, I accept that they're a valid way to get to places that are so deep that they're otherwise impractical. I've watched a motorhead mentality take hold among their users, though, who become more interested in the machine than in the backcountry experience. Magazines and films have helped this along. Designated federal wilderness areas (Mt Rose, Granite Chief, Desolation, Mokelumne, Carson-Iceberg) are all off limits to snowmobiles. Most of Northern Sierra backcountry is open to snowmobiles, so there's no excuse for poaching into restricted areas.

Where I feel sure to draw some justifiable criticism is my rather liberal approach to bestowing names on chutes that have no names known to me. This is a peculiarity of the Northern Sierra – the number of rarely done epic couloirs and their anonymity. I welcome information from people who have done these chutes before me, and their knowledge about any existing names. A number of names were meant as temporary ones to identify the chute in question among friends, though certain ones like Babycham have gained a wider acceptance in the backcountry community.

For the true explorers, I leave you with this thought from Geoffrey Household:

Is the secret of happiness a mixture of passionate fornication and somewhat chancy hunting? If so, we human beings have been continually frustrated by urban life ever since we were fools enough to invent it.

Ben Roy, Carson Pass

Backcountry Safety and Equipment

Before I get into this section, I want to reiterate that these brief highlights are no substitute for experience, knowledge, training, and a copy of *Mountaineering: Freedom of the Hills*. You might think that experience and knowledge amount to the same thing, but believe me, you don't always learn from your mistakes. At the other end, I've found freshly trained people from avalanche classes who are so full of jargon and caution that they're reluctant to go out and test their knowledge. There is always a balance, but there's no getting around one central fact. The backcountry is dangerous. It kills people.

In my early years of doing backcountry, I was resentful of the veterans who wouldn't let you join them unless you had all the gear. I couldn't afford everything I needed, and I thought they were being elitists. The more time I've spent out in questionable conditions and far from help, the more I have been brought around to their point of view, though. When you're out in the backcountry, you never want to be thinking of your partner(s) as a potential liability. You want to be out with people you trust with your life. Though I still go out with almost anyone on short day trips, there are only a few people I trust to go on deep hikes to terrain that I don't know. If you can find a dependable partner early on, you'll be more likely to do serious adventuring.

Tom Burt and Jim Zellers have been one of the premier backcountry mountaineering duos in snowboarding, and their adventures have taken them from their humble beginnings in the Tahoe basin to the Eastern Sierra to the Andes to the Himalayas. They learned each other's limits, trusted completely in each other, and reached a level where they wouldn't contemplate doing a serious adventure with anyone else. Tom told me a comic story of an Andes trip with my friend Jason Schutz, who while now one of the world's more accomplished snowboard mountaineers, was still something of a rookie at the time. They bought a live chicken at a village along the way and toted it up with them. Jason developed altitude sickness at 15,000 feet and left his main pack behind at a forward base camp. When they drew straws over who was going to do the honors of killing the chicken, Jason won. Unfortunately his good knife was back in his main pack. Not only that, he was a vegetarian. He sawed away at the chicken miserably with a pocket knife while Tom and Jim laughed. So don't worry about how inexperienced you are when you get to do a trip with some real veterans. We were all virgins once. You may suffer some humiliation, but you'll take away much more in learning than you lose in pride.

Many people wonder, when they watch film footage of Tahoe backcountry, how the pros decide whether a line is safe to do when the snow is fresh and deep. "Do they throw bombs at it?" "Do they dig a pit?" "Do they just feel it?" The answer is definitely not (a), but more of a combination of (b) and (c). The veterans use some science - a check of the snow layers and likelihood of a slide - years and years of experience in judging the best line and where the islands of safety are, and then finally they ride it twice as fast as many of us are ever likely to do.

Without diminishing the importance of the science, I find that in the Northern Sierra the latter factors weigh more heavily. Partly I say this because the snow stabilizes so rapidly here compared to dry snow areas, and it's easier to watch each storm and have a good idea how the layers have built up. Even if you're a local who knows what kind of layering there is, though, a pit should always be dug because there are factors like windloading and temperature differences due to elevation that can't be computed from the safety of your house. As far as your actual riding, the faster you go and the less turns you do, the less chance there is of setting off a slide, and the more chance you have of getting to your island of safety if you do set one. At the same time, don't ride out of control, because there's nothing like a good tumble to set off a slide and when you're off your feet there's no riding out of it.

In really steep chutes, even heavy Sierra snow has trouble bonding, and I don't know how many times I've watched people jump around in the top of the chute and send all the good powder sloughing out the bottom. Though it's scary to come screaming out of a chute real fast, the snow is likely to be much more pocketed in below it than it is in the chute itself and it's relatively easy to slow down in a deep pile of bottomless powder. Even in crustier conditions it's good to learn to link longer, smoother turns down steeps. Though I used to get in over my head all too often in chutes, I've tried to back off to a policy of where I don't do it unless I know I can do it clean. Jump turning is fine for skiers, but you want to avoid it on a snowboard.

At the other extreme, snowboard and ski films have made straightlining chutes all the new rage. That's nice for guys that have a heli to take them back up, but even then it's often a waste of a good mountain. Not only that, but some of the guys do it to hide the fact that they're lousy at turning on steeps. If you watch big mountain experts like Jeremy Jones and Karleen Jeffery, you see fast and smooth steeps riding at its best.

Dave Frissyn, keeping it pointed down the fall line

There was a fear among avalanche professionals a decade ago that snowboarders were going to be responsible for a major new boost in the statistics, but it hasn't turned out to be the case. Skiers are often more likely to trigger avalanches through cutting deeper turns, whereas snowboarders - especially in Sierra cement - tend to float more on top. In any event, snowmobilers are the ones dropping like flies at the moment. High marking is a great way to cut loose unstable slopes, and there's nothing the power of a snowmobile can do to save you when it happens.

A full avalanche course at somewhere like Sierra College (which has the most on-snow time and a great instructor in Dick Penniman) or Alpine Skills International is where you should ideally start, but failing that at the very least attend a one day avalanche seminar. Ski resorts often conduct free ones, and you can contact one of the places listed below for one close to you. I went to a seminar some years back that was conducted by the Cyberspace Snow and Avalanche Center, and I was surprised how much I got out of it. I wasn't expecting to learn much I didn't know already, but it reinforced some issues I'd gotten lazy about. The main one is there are so many different ways for avalanches to happen, and just because the surface is stable doesn't mean a massive slab won't let go. This is what can happen when the first snow of the season falls before the ground freezes. Instead of a solid bond forming, the entire snowpack builds up over the equivalent of roller bearings.

The slide show the CSAC speaker conducted was the highlight. He had pictures from all over the Northern Sierra backcountry, including many places I knew of but had never been. Even if you have the training, don't dismiss these free seminars as pointless. They're a good refresher and are put on by people who spend their lives in the backcountry, and chances are you'll pick up some clues on some new terrain to check out. The following links are the best sources on for Tahoe backcountry information.

Avalanche Forecasting –
Lake Tahoe/Donner Pass 530-587-2158
Cyberspace Snow and Avalanche Center - www.csac.org
Couloir Online - www.couloirmag.com

Avalanche Training/Seminars –
Alpine Meadows Ski Corp 530-583-4232
PO Box AM, Tahoe City, CA 96145
Alpine Skills International 530-582-9170
11400 Donner Pass Rd, Truckee, CA 96161
Outdoor Adventures 530-752-1995
UC Davis - Sacramento
Peak Adventures 916-278-6321
California State University - Sacramento
REI 510-527-4140
1338 San Pablo Ave, Berkeley, CA 94702
Sierra College 530-587-3849
Truckee Campus

Lodges and Huts–
Sierra Club (Benson Hut, Peter Grubb Hut, Bradley Hut)
www.sierraclub.org 530-426-3632

California Alpine Club (Echo Summit Lodge)
www.calpine.org   415-457-9028

Sierra Ski Touring/Husky Express (Meiss Hut)
http://highsierra.com/sst/ski/meiss.htm   775-782-3047

Topo and Relief Maps – http://tahoe.usgs.gov

Weather - TahoeCam.com   (live cam, weather links, road info)

Jeff Krebill, Meg Pugh, and dog Kaya, Sonora Pass

One of the other things about getting backcountry experience is - as obvious as it seems - you have to go into the backcountry to get it. Because you can drop Chimney Sweep at Squaw Valley doesn't mean you're going to feel comfortable dropping into The Cross on Mt Tallac. It's a whole different world when ski patrol hasn't put its stamp of approval on an area. Even if you do a lot of out of bounds at resorts like Sugar Bowl or Alpine Meadows, you're not accustomed to hiking up the lines you're going to do and getting a feel for snow conditions on the way up. That's why resort-accessed backcountry is often the most dangerous. The avalanche deaths that keep occurring at resorts - both from people legally and illegally skiing out-of-bounds - is testament to this.

Too many people want to develop backcountry skills by osmosis, rather than accept the fact that you have to go out there and grunt, huff, sweat, and occasionally bleed. If you're not out there because you love the wilderness and enjoy hiking, you're probably not meant for the backcountry. When you get into comparing hiking time versus riding time, you're looking at it all wrong. I get that all the time from resort junkies, and even if I didn't enjoy the wilderness aspect, my answer is this: For all their vaunted pleasures, Tahoe resorts can't hold a candle to the lines of Tahoe backcountry.

One of the most important things to keep in mind is that a line never "has to be" ridden. Know when to back off. Most mountaineering deaths on Everest and elsewhere are from people reluctant to turn back when a lifetime dream is in sight. All hikes in the Northern Sierra are fortunately short enough that there is less likelihood of being biased so heavily by the effort you put into getting there. Still, I made the critical mistake once in the Desolation Wilderness backcountry, and escaped with my life only by a freak piece of luck. A good friend and one of the best backcountry skiers I knew in Tahoe, Aaron Martin, was not so lucky. In April of 2002, he misjudged on an adventure to 18,000' Mount St Elias in Alaska, and died along with his friend Reid Sanders. After Aaron's successful mountaineering ascent of Mt Logan, the highest peak in Canada, he had dreamed about the Mount St Elias trip for years. I knew how much it meant to him, and how easy it must have been to convince himself the impossible was possible.

For winter backcountry in the Sierra, my minimal equipment list for a typical day trip includes the basics: backpack, avalanche transceiver, map, shovel, food, plenty of water, sunscreen, eyewear, emergency blanket, poles (that convert into an avalanche probe), and snowshoes. There are a number of items you can add to this, most importantly a navigation device. Other options are an ice ax and crampons – essential if you plan to take on a technical chute in questionable conditions - first aid kit, webbing or 7 mm rope, and a cell phone and/or two-way radios.

The avalanche transceiver has traditionally been the most expensive piece of backcountry gear, and thus many novices have done without. I didn't have one for a number of years until I started doing more winter backcountry, and the death of pro snowboarder Jamil Khan drove home the need to use one all the time. Though they cost a bit ($250-300) and you hope to never use one, the survival rate of people who have been buried less than fifteen minutes is 90 percent. From there it drops off dramatically. Without a beacon to locate someone, it's awfully hard to get them out in less than that time. Besides being expensive, the avalanche transceiver is the most misunderstood piece of backcountry equipment. Many people wear them without a clue how they work, and some I've worked with will try to save room in their pack by wearing a transceiver but leaving their shovel at home. (Hmmm, I know just where my buddy is but I have nothing to dig him out with.) The typical analog transceiver is not as confusing as most people think. Once you pick up a signal, it's just a matter of following the loudest signal directly to the victim, resetting the distance range as you go each time it reaches maximum volume.

Many companies are offering digital transceivers now, which simplify the searching process by giving you the exact distance and direction to the buried victim. You still have to follow the grid search pattern to pick up the signal initially, though. The great advantage is in quickly locating the exact spot the person is buried, which can be confusing with analog transceivers. All avalanche transceivers require training and practice to use effectively, so make sure you have a book or manual to learn from and do as many practice searches with your friends as you can.

Shovels are available from Life-Link, Voile, Da Kine, Ascension, and other companies. They cost $35-40 and come in two main types; smaller bladed plastic ones and larger bladed aluminum ones. Some even come with a snow saw built into the handle, which is useful. Though I like the smaller ones for minimizing pack space, they're not nearly as effective as the aluminum blades for digging through hard chunks of Sierra cement. Also, the larger blades are better for building kickers. So there's a trade-off, space or function? I find that when I start thinking of my tools as merely the minimum required for an emergency, I'm shortchanging myself and my backcountry companions. The plastic blades work great for the majority of conditions, but may fail you when trying to dig through the rubble of a broken cornice. Also, you're fighting time and panic when you're trying to dig someone out and you want maximum efficiency. This all being said, I've been using plastic blades for the last few seasons, so it's a personal choice. (You may find yourself losing friends, though, if they catch on to the fact that they only rate a plastic blade.)

The topographical map, or topo, is a staple of backcountry travel. Combined with a handheld GPS, you can navigate through the worst of blizzard conditions and have an exact fix on where you are. Because GPS units receive signals from satellites, though, they don't work in forest cover or anywhere you have obstruction of the whole range of sky. (While a luxury, GPS units can be bought for as little as $99 these days and are a joy for areas you're unfamiliar with.)

If you don't have experience reading topo contour lines, it's worth spending awhile comparing a topo map to mountains you are familiar with and learning all the subtleties of topo map reading. It will save you a good deal of time on route finding and trip planning. Because the standard 7.5 minute topo only covers an area of 6.6 miles by 6.6 miles, you'll find yourself spending an awful lot of money at $4 a pop if you're exploring a lot. Often the area you're interested in is on the corner of a map, and you have to piece two or three together to see everything. This is where topo maps on CD-ROM come in handy. You can buy a CD-ROM for your computer that has all the topo maps of the Northern Sierra region on one disk. Different companies sell these CD's for about $50 in most back-country stores of Northern California. There are a pile of added benefits to

CD topos, like being able to zoom in on sections, view in relief form, or plot elevation gain of a hike.

The USGS has an amazing online topo map tool that can be found at **http://tahoe.usgs.gov/DRG.html** for the whole Tahoe region from Truckee south to Echo Summit. It's a joy if you have a high speed internet connection. The USGS Tahoe website which this is contained in – tahoe.usgs.gov – is an incredible resource for map fans and those looking to learn more about topography and bathymetry of the Lake Tahoe region.

Though you hate to plan for it, you want to be ready on a basic level for a really nasty injury to happen. An emergency blanket - 5'x7' sheets of reflective foil that only weigh 3 oz - and a fleece jacket are always good to carry. A first aid kit and a companion with EMT training is ideal, but failing that you want to stay warm while your friend gets help.

Tahoe being so mild compared to most places, I usually hike in a polypro shirt and if it's really windy or storming I'll wear my shell. As hot as you get hiking, don't think it means you can carry less. Always pack at least a shell for when you get up top, because before you know it you'll be standing on a wind-blasted ridge freezing your ass off when you were sweating just five minutes before.

The author displays fashion at Grouse Rock and practicality on Mt Tallac.

Being the fashion pigs we humans are, I often see guys hiking in their favorite cotton t-shirts and sweatshirts. I learned long ago this is a recipe for misery. Cotton holds moisture by the skin and you end up with a soaked, freezing shirt when you stop hiking and cool down. Synthetic microfibers wick the moisture to the outside of the fabric and keep your skin dry. Polyester fleece is a prime example of this. Any kayaker that has had to swim in a freezing river can tell you nothing beats fleece for keeping you warm and dry when the fabric is full of water.

In the wet snow of the Sierra, good waterproof clothing is key. Clothing is a personal thing, but if you're looking at it purely in terms of function, I'd suggest looking more toward the mountaineering and backcountry companies. Most snowboard and ski clothing companies do make an excellent top-of-the-line series, but it's no cheaper than Mountain Hardwear, Lowe Alpine, or Marmot. I place my faith in dryness a lot more readily in companies that have been designing for many years for the worst mountain conditions in the world. While GoreTex has traditionally been the standard in high quality stormwear, most mountaineering companies have an equivalent material that is just as good. I've found that a quality storm shell rarely retails for less than $300, though they can sometimes be bought for half that at clearance sales.

A big safety change that I watched take place in the past decade was the move to wearing helmets. Though most of the photos in this book are shot before helmets really became popular, almost everyone I know is riding with one now. Having noggin protection can be the difference between life and death in a slide-for-life down a chute, or when riding fast through trees. Plus they keep your ears warm. Plenty of companies make them – Boeri, Red, Leedom, ProTec – and I highly recommend using one.

Adam Hostetter   Erik Wilhelm

Snowshoes used to be a clunky luxury afforded by the fortunate few, but there was something of a revolution five or six years ago. The biggest leap forward in backcountry access was Pete Carney introducing the Verts snowshoe. It's a ridiculously simple plastic design that has transformed deep powder climbing from a posthole nightmare to a stair-step breeze. They are the ultimate snowshoe for hiking steeps, and work fine with both snowboard and ski boots. Redfeather and Atlas make good, light shoes with solid, ratchet binding systems and crampons, but at considerable more expense. They sidehill traverse much better than the Verts, but aren't as good on serious steeps. MSR makes a nice, inexpensive plastic shoe with a crampon, and Tubbs makes some affordable shoes as well.

A controversy to be avoided is the skin vs snowshoe conflict (not to be confused with the skin vs mohawk conflict, which is something else entirely, and since I think Glen Plake's an alright guy, there's no reason we can't all get along). This potential ugliness is caused by many snowboarders new to the backcountry - and some skiers - blithely ruining the skin tracks of a skier by stomping right up them. A basic rule of thumb is to always respect the hard work someone put in to make the first tracks up a peak. Unless a skin track is packed down hard and you can't damage it, establish a separate snowshoe track.

Most casual backcountry snowboarders consider hiking poles an unnecessary item, but if you're doing serious hiking they're well worth investing in. The improved balance leads to greater hiking speed, and using your arms to help you climb makes life on your legs easier. Life-Link makes a variety of superlight, 2 part, collapsible poles, and Leki and Rossignol make 3 part designs that collapse shorter but are heavier. Most can convert to avalanche probes, which is essential unless you're carrying a separate avalanche probe with you. Even if they do, you might want to consider carrying an avalanche probe because when you're in a rush to find a buried friend - and speed is of the essence - you don't want to waste time frantically trying to get your poles apart and screwed back together into a probe. Again, there's no use having a transceiver unless you can quickly pinpoint the location of the victim.

The ever-growing popularity of split boards is the most recent revolution in backcountry access. For a number of years Voile has been tinkering with and improving on the split board concept until they have created a system that works pretty well in a variety of conditions. For those unfamiliar with the concept, the split board splits down the middle so that each half can be used as climbing skis. Climbing skins fit the base of the skis to give you exceptional traction while ascending pitches, and the bonus is that the skis are so wide that they don't sink in deep powder as much as traditional skis do. When you get to the summit, the bindings rotate around sideways, the board clips solidly together, and you've got a snowboard. For once, instead of being left far behind telemarkers on long ascents, snowboarders can lead the way. Jim Zellers uses his split board religiously for fast ascents. Dave Downing has put the Burton split board to great use, proving its versatility with his hard riding. The downside is price - expect to pay $800-1000 for the whole package.

Though split boards make ultimate sense for minimizing a snowboarder's gear, I'm still not entirely sold on them. Joining them can sometimes be a chore, and they'll never be quite what a regular board is. Also, you're limited to the designs offered by Voile and Burton. Still, my friends who use split boards swear by them. Their superiority is in deep powder, where the huge surface area keeps you afloat on ascents, and any limitations of the board are unnoticeable in riding the fluff downhill. For mixed conditions, or shallow powder, approach skis can be the ticket. I used my own home-made set for a few years, but now K2 markets some. At only 108cm long, they strap on to your backpack for the descent without being especially cumbersome. While not boasting much more surface area than snowshoes, they traverse better, glide over flats, and you can follow existing skin tracks that skiers have set.

If you're an alpine skier, of course, few of those choices concern you. A set of climbing skins and randoneé/touring bindings and you're set to go in most conditions. The exception is hiking steeps in powder, where there's nothing simpler or more effective than a pair of Verts.

Finally, this brings us to what to pack all this gear in; the backpack. There are so many good ones on the market that it's a personal choice. The ideal day pack is between 1800-2800 cubic inches, with an internal frame, shovel holder, top compartment, hydration bladder, and a snowboard sling for riders, or straps to hold your skis securely. Something pack makers didn't comprehend for years – and many still don't – is that we don't want to hike with our board or skis four feet above our heads. Slings and ski holders too often don't let you lower the vertical space you take up, and hiking through trees becomes a nightmare. More snowboard pack makers are recognizing this, and avoiding slings in favor of rubberized straps that hold the board between the bindings, letting it ride lower on you. The rails of the board quickly cut through regular webbing straps, so make sure to get straps specifically designed to prevent that.

Tahoe Basin

My introduction to the Tahoe backcountry came shortly after moving to the lake in 1991. Since I was living on the West Shore, the peaks of Ward Valley and Blackwood Canyon were the most accessible, with Twin Peaks and Fourth of July Chutes being my first real challenges. My friend James and I drove his '57 Chevy as far up the road to Barker Pass as we could in the early season, and as soon as it got stuck in the snow we hiked up to Fourth of July from there.

I steadily moved farther afield. Hiking the chutes above Emerald Bay and the Galena Bowls of Mount Rose backcountry, I picked up tips and knowledge as I went. It wasn't for about four or five years that I did much winter backcountry, reasoning that without an avalanche transceiver it would be foolish. Winter in Tahoe never ceased to amaze me, though. Every day I drove to work at Dave's Ski Shop in Tahoe City those first few years, I just stared across the lake and marveled at the beauty of the place. In all my travels throughout the world to that point, I hadn't been anywhere that so constantly awed me. Mark Twain felt the same way, writing in his 1864 book *Roughing It*:

"The forest about us was dense and cool, the sky above us was cloudless and brilliant with sunshine, the broad lake before us was glassy and clear, or rippled and breezy, or black and storm-tossed, according to Nature's mood; and its circling border of mountain domes, clothed with forests, scarred with land-slides, cloven by cannons and valleys, and helmeted with glittering snow, fitly framed and finished the noble picture. The view was always fascinating, bewitching, entrancing."

The more short day trips I did around the lake, the more impressed I was at how much endless variety of terrain there seemed to be. Once I had a fair bit under my belt, I started buying topo maps and pestering veterans for info on new places to go. What I soon noticed was how set a lot of casual backcountry skiers were in their routines. On one particular spring trip to Jake's, there were moguls on one face it had been skied so much. Only a quarter mile away on the ridge there were scarcely any tracks at all.

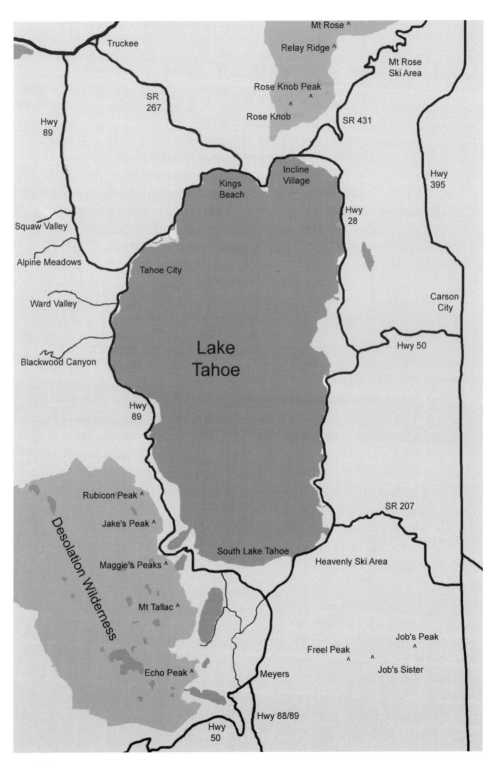

I became somewhat obsessed with learning as much about the Tahoe backcountry as I could. The vast bulk of it saw incredibly few people, considering that the region is used more heavily by backcountry snowboarders and skiers than anywhere else in the United States. What I found was that few locals seemed to be aware of the depth of what was in their backyard. Serious backcountry mountaineers kept telling me I needed to take the next step and go down to the real peaks of the Southern Sierra.

A transition was taking place, though, in which I became a devoted winter powder pig. Every season I couldn't bear to watch the snow rot out in spring and the mountains melt to brown, nor did corn snow hold its allure anymore. Down south was very much a springtime place, I gathered. Eventually I stopped even snowboarding at the resorts, unwilling to deal with the zoo-like atmosphere and the desperate scramble to get fresh tracks in the first half hour of a powder day. No matter what the conditions, somewhere in the Tahoe backcountry was almost always holding good untracked snow. Raining to the top of Squaw Valley? Mt Rose would have powder. A huge fresh snowfall with too much avalanche danger? The tree runs of Rubicon, Jake's, and east of Alpine Meadows were usually safe. Sunbaked a few days later? (All it takes is one day in Tahoe's balmy winter weather, more often than not.) The north face of Maggie's or some of the chutes on Tallac would be shaded and fresh. In need of escaping from humanity as far and as quickly as possible? Desolation Wilderness beckoned.

Unlike the typical mountaineer, I never had an urge to bag the biggest classics, the highest peaks. I wanted the most fun and accessible conditions and best snow. The more I adventured, the more I realized what an extraordinary place the Tahoe Basin was for winter backcountry riding. Substitute "backcountry" for "lakes" in this Mark Twain quote, and you get my feelings on the place.

"I measure all lakes by Tahoe, partly because I am far more familiar with it than with any other, and partly because I have such a high admiration for it and such a world of pleasant recollections of it, that it is very nearly impossible for me to speak of lakes and not mention it."

Because I have a terrible sense of direction, an unfortunate curse for an explorer, I made a point of studying the peaks in every direction when I was on top of one. It took quite a few years, but eventually I could name all the major peaks within sight, and recognize them from all sides. As much as anything, this contributed to my sense of comfort and familiarity. Once the entire basin became my playground, nothing seemed particularly daunting or out of reach anymore. I knew I had reached an important point when I felt this way about Desolation Wilderness, which to most people is hopelessly intimidating in its size. Unfortunately, just because you think you can cross valleys like a giant with a single stride, the realities of distance do beat you down every so often.

A man who was utterly unfazed by distance was John "Snowshoe" Thompson, the first Tahoe backcountry skier and the grandfather of skiing in the United States. This adventurous Norwegian was living in the Sierra foothills in 1856 when he read that the people of Genoa in the Carson Valley had not received mail for months, isolated by the winter snows.

Responding to the challenge, he made a pair of skis for himself that were modeled on the traditional Norwegian snow skates he had used in his youth, long planks that weighed twenty-five pounds. The townspeople thought him even crazy when they watched him train on them. Because no one had ever heard of a snow skate before, they decided they were just some newfangled form of snowshoe and he was promptly nicknamed "Snowshoe" Thompson.

When he was sure of his abilities, he approached the postmaster at Placerville, and offered to establish regular service across the mountains, by "snow skates" in the winter and horseback in the summer. It was ninety miles from Placerville to Genoa, through a frozen wilderness. Word got out of his daring plan and the townspeople of Placerville thought him even crazier. The brutal fate of the Donner Party to the north of Lake Tahoe was very fresh in people's minds, having happened less than a decade before. Thompson reasoned that he could navigate during the day by the moss that grew on the north side of rocks and trees, and by the stars at night. If all went well, he would make the trip in three days. On the face of it his plan did seem relatively insane. With no more than beef jerky and biscuits, along with a mackinaw jacket over his shirt, he strapped on the eighty pound mail bag and set out on a January morning.

Midway through the journey, a powerful storm swept through and obliterated his ability to navigate. Nevertheless, his sense of direction was so good that he carried on and eventually came out on the south shore of Lake Tahoe, just as he had planned. He used pine needles for bedding along the way, and lit fallen or leaning trees on fire to keep warm.

just how puny we are – Dave Frissyn as a speck hiking the upper part of Mt Tallac

Crossing Luther Pass below the south end of the lake, he came down into Woodfords Canyon and the west fork of the Carson River. He knew he was homefree at this point, and followed the river downhill and around to the base of Job's Peak, and into the valley to the stockade town of Genoa.

The people of Genoa were as astounded as the folks of Placerville had been doubtful. Few dared to cross the Sierra at all in a heavy winter, but what kind of superman did it take to do it in three days? The legend of Snowshoe Thompson was born. A day later he began his return trip to Placerville with the mail, and regularly did the roundtrip in future months in five days – three days up and two days back. His routes expanded, carrying supplies back and forth to the miners in Virginia City as well. His expertise on his skis was a source of wonder for people, who gathered to watch him come flying down slopes and launch into the air. Twenty years later, at the first ski jumping competition, people still weren't matching the lengths of his early efforts on his crude snow skates. (Thanks to David Beck at Sierra Ski Tours for the Thompson info.)

Thompson was not the first of the trans-Sierran mail carriers, as he is often credited for. That honor belonged to John Calhoun Johnson, who discovered the Johnson Pass route that Thompson used through the Sierra to save considerable time from the Carson Valley to Placerville and Sacramento. Johnson Pass lies a mile to the north of Echo Summit on Highway 50, and was the old pass before Highway 50 altered the route in the 1940's. The Johnson Pass route was a huge improvement over the trans-Sierran route of Kit Carson, which was a long detour to the south over Carson Pass and much higher terrain. Still, it was Snowshoe Thompson who revolutionized winter travel in the Northern Sierra, and inspired others to try out his strange way of sliding across the snow.

Because Samuel Clemens arrived in the Carson Valley in the early 1860's, it's conceivable that Thompson carried mail of the writer soon to be known as Mark Twain. Where Thompson impressed the people of the Carson Valley with his physical prowess, Clemens made an immediate impression with his strange clothing and odd behavior. His brother had been appointed Secretary of Nevada and the young Samuel duly appointed himself to the unpaid position of private secretary to the Secretary. Albert Bigelow wrote in his 1912 biography of Twain:

"Lately a river sovereign and dandy, in fancy percales and patent leathers, he had become the roughest of rough-clad pioneers, in rusty slouch hat, flannel shirt, coarse trousers slopping half in and half out of the heavy cowskin boots. Always something of a barbarian in love with the loose habit of unconvention, he went even further than others and became a sort of paragon of disarray. The more energetic citizens of Carson did not prophesy much for his future among them."

Twain did not get caught up in gold rush fever right away, but more immediately became entranced with Lake Tahoe. Along with his brother, he staked out a timber claim and loosely fenced off a plot of land. Though it showed some ambition on his part, it was mostly an excuse to indulge in the beauty of the lake. He wrote in *Roughing It*:

"That morning we could have whipped ten such people as we were the day before -- sick ones at any rate. But the world is slow, and people will go to "water cures" and "movement cures" and to foreign lands for health. Three months of camp life on Lake Tahoe would restore an Egyptian mummy to his pristine vigor, and give him an appetite like an alligator. I do not mean the oldest and driest mummies, of course, but the fresher ones. The air up there in the clouds is very pure and fine, bracing and delicious. And why shouldn't it be? -- it is the same the angels breathe. I think that hardly any amount of fatigue can be gathered together that a man cannot sleep off in one night on the sand by its side."

There are few more entertaining accounts of life in the pioneer days of the Northern Sierra than can be found in *Roughing It*. Twain captures the beauty of the unspoiled paradise it was with the fervor of a Romantic poet, and describes his various misadventures with the humor of the best travel writers. Though he was fairly young – or perhaps because of it - the writing is Twain at his absolute best. I'm not sure why it isn't more well known as one of his classics, but it should be. If you need some reading material for a backcountry camping trip, definitely pick up a copy of it.

Ward Valley

Most of the descents of Ward Valley fall into the realm of Alpine Meadows accessed backcountry, but eventually the terrain becomes a whole different area. A major problem with accessing all this terrain through anywhere but Alpine Meadows is that there's no legal parking on the Sherwood Chair side of the mountain, making it awfully difficult to hike. Grouse Rock is the farthest out you can go on High Traverse and still ride back to the Sherwood lift, but the ridge between Ward Peak and Grouse is only for resort powder pigs obsessed with fresh tracks. If I'm going out that way at all, I'm going on beyond. Grouse Rock will always have sentimental value as being the first backcountry I did in Tahoe in my days of learning how to snowboard, but that says something about it in itself. If you opt to follow the ridge line from Grouse Rock back toward Twin Peaks, you come across some fun chutes and spines in a zone known as Little Alaska. It's long been a favorite of filmers, though one pro snowboarder severely injured himself here while filming and had to be helicoptered out.

Erik Wilhelm, Little Alaska

Dave Frissyn, Little Alaska

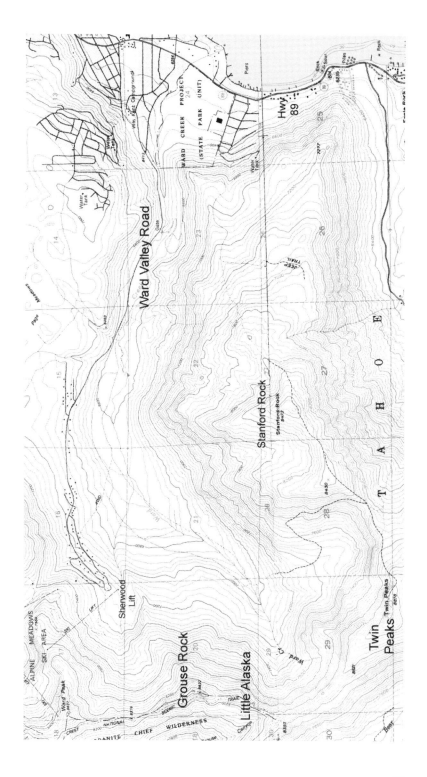

29

Little Alaska

Farther out on the ridge is a cliff with one reasonably do-able chute on skier's left, and a dogleg piece of sickness in the middle that's not so bad if you can figure a way to drop in. Freeski legend Shane McConkey has apparently belayed into it, from which it's just a pointer. Dave Downing has also ridden it.

Twin Peaks (8878') is accessible by hiking the ridge around the backside of the two prongs. A couple of easy chute entries lie between the two peaks, quickly giving way to a wide open bowl. If the winter's been a big one, the face of the north peak will be covered and you can actually drop from the top of it, but we're talking about something well over a 50 degree pitch. Down toward the bottom of the bowl is the famous Twin Peaks windlip, seen in some of the early 90's snowboard videos with Steve Graham, Damian Sanders, and Noah Salasnek hucking large off it. They cross-country skied up one of the forest roads through the valley and then hiked up, but doing it via the ridge is just as easy and you get the descent, too. It's one of the best natural windlips around Tahoe, and beyond smoothing the run-in, there's not a thing you have to do to build it up. It goes over a twenty foot table top and drops away down a great landing slope, with big air time if you're willing to hit it fast enough.

Getting out from Twin Peaks is the interesting part. The first time I hiked it, we took four hours to get back there and another five to get out. We ended up in the valley following one of the forest roads, not realizing that it was paralleling Ward Valley Road rather than taking us out to it. Totally lost, we finally struggled out amidst some homes way down the road from our car. The best way is to ride down from the windlip, bearing left continually until it flattens out. Then hike across the valley (north) until you get to Grouse Ridge, climb on top of it and ride down toward Sherwood Chair.

Twin Peaks in a big snow year - the face of the north peak is filled in

It's easy to get lost in the valley if you're not familiar with it, so don't go out there unless you're with someone who is. Rachael Woods, who works at Alpine Meadows, told me of going out to Little Alaska with five people one day. One of them was supposed to meet them out there, never showed, and they found her three hours later postholing miserably toward Lake Tahoe through waist deep snow on the valley floor.

On top of the south wall of Ward Valley is Stanford Rock (8473'), which is a popular mountain biking trail in summer but little known as a backcountry snow destination. You can see Stanford Rock from Tahoe City as you look straight down the road, a rock cliff over an open run of snow that disappears into trees lower down. When you get up to the top of Stanford Rock, you get one of the finer views of the lake from any of the basin's peaks. I used to drag people up there because it's a good photo shoot spot, but it's by no means worth it just for the terrain.

You can get some good turns in the open bowl for a few hundred yards beneath the rock, but then the trees get thick. There may be a tree run down the fall line to Ward Creek, but I've never gone that way. I always return more or less the way I came up, just so I can get straight back to the car. It's awfully flat most of the way, though there is a steep gully run right at the end. Stanford Rock is backcountry best suited to touring skiers, but it's one of the more beautiful hikes you can do. I've seen bears, coyotes, and golden eagles up there.

Liz McMillan, Stanford Rock

Way out in the wilderness behind Twin Peaks is a legendary cirque seen in many a snowboard film, known as Sunken Meadow. There are beautiful cliffs and steep landing transitions, and every size huck imaginable is there for the taking. Most film crews get back there by snowmobile through Blackwood Canyon, but they're skirting the edge of legality. The meadow is within the Granite Chief Wilderness, and snowmobile access is only legal as far as a nearby ridge.

Sunken Meadow

Blackwood Canyon

Aside from the short descents off the side of the Stanford Ridge, there aren't too many reasons to go back up Blackwood Canyon. Snowmobile traffic is heavy in winter, and unless you're on one you'll be choking down exhaust from ones passing you. One good destination is the Fourth of July chutes, which are north facing, steep, and respectable for Tahoe couloirs. Because Blackwood Canyon Road is closed during the winter, they're not done much by hikers except in late spring/summer. Most people wait until the road is open all the way to the top of Barker Pass, and then it's less than a half hour hike back to the chutes. Early season and late season are best, because in mid-winter the chutes fill in too much to be nearly as challenging.

By the time the snow's gone from everywhere else (say, the Fourth of July), a couple of the chutes are still filled in and become pretty popular. When I first met Erik Wilhelm in the summer of '95, I took him back there. After sampling each of the two main chutes, he exclaimed:

"This is better than Squaw was two months ago!"

mid-winter Fourth of July Chutes

A nearby skier muttered, "Yeah, and there are more people here than there were at Squaw two months ago."

When Homewood opened up a pretty much full-time backcountry gate to Ellis Peak in the late 90's, the backcountry out here became a lot more accessible in winter. Fourth of July is still a long way out along the ridges, even by split board or skis, but possible. (Think along the lines of hiking out to Twin Peaks from the Alpine Meadows boundaries). Not quite so far, there are some good chute and cliff lines between Ellis Peak and Fourth of July, off the west face of Ellis Peak. The 1200' descent takes you down into a creek gully and across some flats to Blackwood Canyon Road, but then it's a long ski out. Best to stay up above the trees, and hike back up to Ellis Peak again and back into Homewood. The descent from Ellis Peak to Lake Louise is one of the basin's classic tree runs.

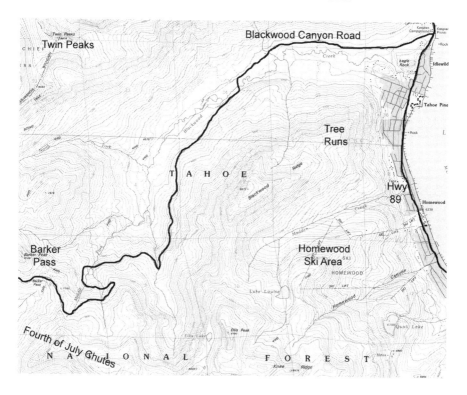

Something to think about for the budget backcountry powder lover is the Homewood early season price on a midweek pass. During June and

July, they offer Mon-Thur passes for the next season for the unbelievable price of $99, and Mon-Fri passes can be purchased through August for only $199. You don't get lift-accessed backcountry cheaper than that.

There are some steep tree shots of about 1000' of vertical out by the lake on the south boundary of Blackwood Canyon, which I did frequently one year when it was my backyard. They're fast and steep, and can be accessed through the Tahoe Pines neighborhood. The snow got so heavy that year that a housemate's car got completely buried in mid-driveway with mine stuck at the top, leaving all four of us in the house to get rides in Brenda's truck, take the bus, or hitch.

Not having a pass to any resort and forced to make do with what I had nearby, I spent most deep powder days trekking up the hill behind the house. To my pleasant surprise I discovered that I lived at the base of the best lakefront tree runs between Tahoe City and Rubicon Peak. Our group poverty was such that Erik Wilhelm thought we lived close enough to Homewood that if he climbed up our hill, he should be able to traverse over to the base of the Madden Lift and save himself a lift ticket. We were divided by more ridges than he realized, and hours of climbing up and down gullies in waist deep snow cured him of ever trying that again.

Brenda Ernst, east end of Blackwood Canyon

Rubicon Peak

Rubicon Peak (9183') is one of the more popular backcountry descents around the basin, though it is mostly done by telemarkers. One of the best tree runs around Tahoe, it's a beefy one with 2400' of vertical. The problem is that it is just that. There aren't many snowboarders or alpine skiers I know who can justify that kind of hike for a tree run, especially when steeper and better terrain is minutes away. The other discouraging thing about Rubicon is the parking situation. It used to be cool to park at the top of the residential neighborhood, but in the '99-'00 winter, cars began to get ticketed and towed because of people parking illegally. As it stands now, there is still no legal parking up there. It cannot be emphasized enough how much care needs to be taken in parking legally in residential neighborhoods where access is dependent upon the goodwill

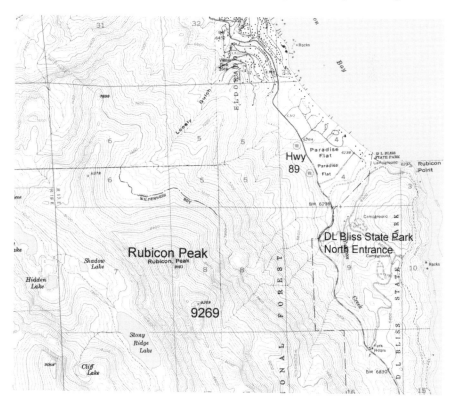

of the residents. In the words of one Rubicon regular:

"Access is not an inalienable right. Don't park in the way of the plows! Stay behind the snow stakes. In full winter that includes not just the initial plowing, but also the subsequent blowing back of the berms. If someone was parking in my neighborhood, blocking the plows from properly clearing the street, I'd be tempted to call the sheriff too. We don't live in a vacuum. Backcountry adventure may be about freedom but it must also be about responsibility. So let's not shit where we play."

Heading south on the West Shore, Rubicon is the first peak on Stony Ridge, a line of nine granders that starts beyond Meeks Bay. The rock nipple on top defines it, which is actually a sheer 100' cliff face. There's almost always a track to follow, because it's one of the first places people go on powder days that are too unstable for anywhere else. The ride back down is the tricky part, because if you follow the fall line you'll end up lost between one of the neighborhoods and the highway. Until you're familiar with it, you're best off staying close to the climbing tracks. DON'T ride back and forth across them, and if you posthole or snowshoe up the skin tracks here, you will face the wrath of Sam, Mark, or half a dozen other telemarkers I know.

Some high quality, rarely ridden terrain is available to the adventurous if you head south from Rubicon Peak along the ridge toward the next peak, 9269'. Why 9269' doesn't get a name is a little curious, since it's the highest peak on Stony Ridge. The bowl that these two peaks anchor is littered with cliff bands, and the powder stays good for a long time. The exit is difficult, and you'll probably find yourself fighting through dense trees toward the bottom before you eventually come out at Hwy 89.

With both Rubicon and Jake's suffering from parking problems and overcrowding, though, it's worth seeing if anywhere around the north entrance to DL Bliss State Park is plowed and open for parking. Just south of the entrance is a gully that runs all the way up to the climber's left side of the 9269' peak. The attraction to many of Rubicon was that the neighborhood parking got you up to 6800'. But once you get down to DL Bliss, Highway 89 reaches this elevation, and no one ever seems to ski the great terrain of 9269'.

Jake's Peak

For big, steep, lakefront descents, Jake's (9187') stands right up there with Tallac as one of the most popular peaks of Tahoe backcountry. Because it's near the road and one of the safest peaks to do on fresh powder days, it has become a subject of controversy in talks of backcountry getting overcrowded. On any nice day in the winter or spring, there will be a half dozen cars in either parking area first thing in the morning. The majority tend to be skiers, since the hike is a little too brutal for the average side-of-the-road snowboarder, and the terrain is mostly

Jaison LeRoy

steep powder runs. A couple of the same guys establish the first trail almost every time, a skin track, and they and the rest of the skiers do not look fondly upon snowshoers and boot hikers destroying it. If you're the first non-skinner up, make your own trail.

With a wealth of descent lines and 2500' of vertical, for all the talk of overcrowding, many of the Jake's descent routes rarely get done. The situation is similar to Tallac, where piles of people hike it yet most of them do North Bowl. I've hardly ever seen a powder track in Emerald Chute, or any of the south face chutes. At the other extreme, in the spring some lines get skied so much they get bumps on them.

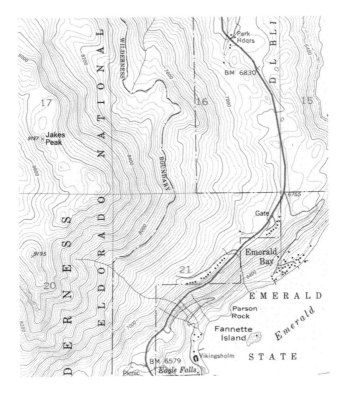

On powder days, the north side tree runs are favored. Like Rubicon, they're some of the safest, long steeps to do when avalanche danger is high elsewhere. In early season, the tree runs are littered with boulders to air but these disappear as it fills in.

North on the ridge from Jake's is a hidden cirque with a challenging set of cliff and chute lines that see very few people. It's worth veering off the normal ascent route and hiking up under it to study the layout. I hiked to it along the ridge the first time, and was unable to make out which descent routes dead-ended in cliffs and which did not. The narrow u-tube chute on skier's far right of the cirque is one of the best lines, with a 10-15' mandatory air out the bottom. In the middle of the cirque there's a chute that is open all the way through, but the rollover is intimidating if you have no idea what's below. Scout what you're not sure about. Unless you exit back toward the ascent route from here, you get stuck in some horribly dense tree descents that aren't much fun.

The other side of Jake's, on the way to Emerald Chute, contains a fine cirque of cliffs, chutes, and trees facing Emerald Bay. Chances are, most of the Tahoe postcards you've seen of skiers and boarders above Emerald Bay were shot up here. On the south-facing slopes are some wide 40 degree chutes and open bowl runs, and the east-facing lines are laden with more trees and rock drops. The south-facing chutes were my early stomping grounds for spring backcountry, because they're steep enough to be a challenge to a novice, but have forgiving corn snow by mid-morning.

Dave Frissyn, Avalanche Gully

Following the ridge out to the southwest, there's a big chute that divides the previous terrain from Emerald Chute. If you're on the way out to the latter, you have to remember this one isn't it. I had a comic radio session with Dave Frissyn one day, as I perched on the other side of Emerald Bay with my large telephoto. He was making sure he was atop Emerald Chute, and he described it closely enough that I was fairly sure he was there, even though I couldn't see him. Finally I told him to go, and waited for him to appear, to no avail. The next thing I knew, a sheepish Dave radioed: "Well, that wasn't the right chute, but it sure was fun."

Because of the sun-baked face, Emerald Chute is actually a rather tricky beast to catch in optimal conditions. A lot of snow is needed to fill it in properly. You don't want to jump on it too quickly after a fresh snow because of avalanche danger, but leave it for a day in the sun and the powder will be gone. The best bet is a day or two after fresh snow, when the weather has remained overcast and cold.

Emerald Chute, 2300' top to bottom

Maggie's Peaks

As you drive around the south side of Emerald Bay, a pair of peaks loom up just above you. These are Maggie's Peaks (8499' and 8699'), the name being a rather obvious allusion to a gal who had an impressive pair. There's a reference in Steinbeck's *Log from the Sea of Cortez* to a pair of Sierra peaks named Maggie's Bubs, and I can only assume these are the same.

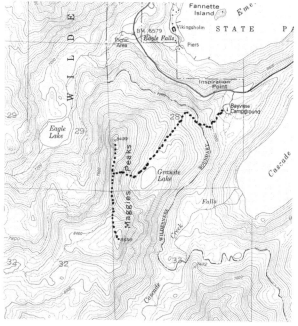

Tom Burt turned me on to a passage from that fine Steinbeck book, which are words every backcountry enthusiast should live by.

"We must remember three things. Number one and first in importance, we must have as much fun as we can with what we have. Number two, we must eat as well as we can, because if we don't, we won't have the health and strength to have as much fun as we might. Number three, and third and last in importance, we must keep the house reasonably in order, wash the dishes and such things. But we will not let the last interfere with the other two."

The north peak of Maggie's is a steep, rock-laden tree run that holds powder for ages after a storm, and the chute entrance up top is a thrill. The best line down it is to end up on the Eagle Falls trail so that you don't get stranded on a steep face overlooking a twenty foot drop to pavement on Hwy 89. Down the east face under the saddle is a mellower tree run down to a lake. On the south peak there are some hairy south face chutes that need tons of snow to fill in properly, and a nice avalanche gully running toward the Cascade Falls trail.

Jamie Scheckman, north peak of Maggie's   (Photo: Grant Barta)

Mt Tallac

Though a few of Tahoe's resorts – such as Squaw Valley and Kirkwood - boast some impressive short sections of steeps terrain, it has always been a given that riders in search of big relentless steeps have to go elsewhere to satisfy their cravings. Because of the relatively puny size of the Northern Sierra mountains compared to their southern counterparts, most Tahoe locals don't get to ride a lot of you-lose-it-you-die steeps. One of the few places to find them around Tahoe is Mt Tallac (9735').

Looming up on the edge of the lake just outside of South Lake Tahoe, Tallac claims 3300' of vertical and enough different technical lines to satisfy the most serious diehards. The Washoe Indian name means, aptly enough, "great mountain". More than steeps, Tallac also is a natural fun park of bowls, windlips, and gullies that make it a joy for people with the stamina to make the grueling hike. The descent from the top of Tallac is continuous and fast for the better part of three thousand feet, though it's the upper half that contains all the best terrain.

I had heard a lot of horror stories of 3-4 hour hikes before I did it for the first time, but it took me just over two hours. When I got my first look at The Cross, which refers to a whole section of the mountain but more commonly means just the chute in the upper arm, butterflies raced through me. It was *steep*. Not only that, it was one of the longest chutes I had seen at the time. You couldn't take the typical Tahoe approach of throwing a few turns and then straightlining into an open bowl. It was a few years before I got the right conditions, and rode the chute from the top. It seemed fairly reasonable in powder but it still scares the hell out of me when I look down it on an icy day.

During the course of my next few trips, I watched a few people try some tricky lines to skier's immediate left of the main chute entry. They were scary just to watch. Of three people I watched attempt these mini-chutes, one skier got frozen for a half hour when confronted with a straight line down salt and pepper rocks, another skier slid out his second turn and went down head first, and a snowboarder nailed a line cleanly. A telemarker I know once watched a friend bounce and slide down the entire length of The Cross, finally spit out the bottom like a rag doll. Pure comedy because he was alright, but not so funny otherwise.

The majority who play it safe come down an open bowl on skier's far left, and enter into the easier part of the chute above a cluster of trees. Tallac doesn't have to be do or die, though. The whole south side of the mountain is a playland with infinite possibilities and an incredible view of the lake. If you don't want to take on The Cross, there's a relatively easy but steep bowl descent off the skier's right side of North Bowl just before it drops into the front mountain chutes. A small cornice builds up, so often you have to air into it. From here you can still access all the windlips, rocks, and mini-chutes of the south side. You can also follow the traditional North Bowl descent to the left of the front mountain chutes, which 90 percent of Tallac hikers do, but it's pretty mellow and lacks features.

Erik Wilhelm, chicken salad stiffie in the fun zone of Tallac

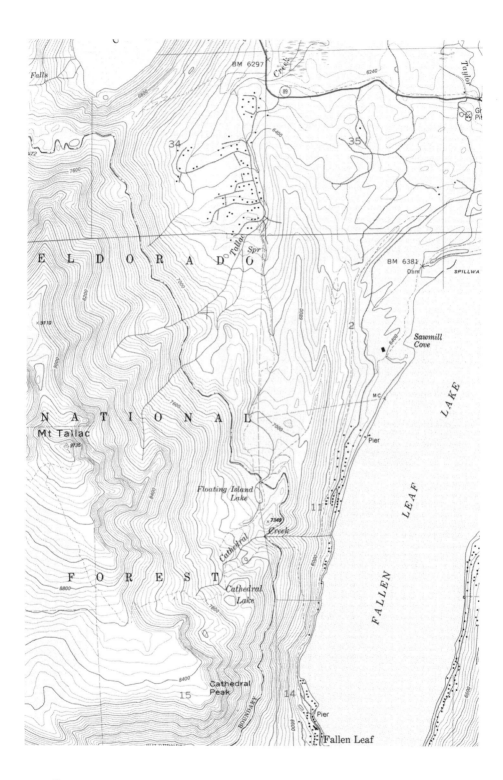

The south side that drops down to Fallen Leaf Lake has all kinds of terrain, but it's a bit of a hassle to get out of there. It's possible to session some of the chutes and cliffs of South Bowl (also known as Cathedral Bowl by some), though, and still hike around a short distance to the SE cirque and be able to ride out the frontside. The SE cirque has at least one substantial chute, which is formed on one side by a gigantic rock cliff that makes you feel very insignificant in its shadow. It takes a while to fill in, though, and often the only opening from the upper bowl to the lower

SE cirque chutes. The chutes coming down from the crossarm of The Cross are in the upper right of the frame. The only dependable way through to the lower bowl is through the short, straight chute in the lower middle.

bowl is a short and steep chute to skier's left of it.

Some of the least known chutes are the ones that drop into the lower bowl from the crossarm of The Cross (i.e, you turn right as soon as you exit the main chute of The Cross.) They're reasonably steep and they dogleg so you can't see the exit, but they turn out to be a relief after the sphincter-clinching descent of the upper mountain.

Dave Frissyn, in two of the chutes from the previous page

If you do ride down the Cathedral Plateau toward Fallen Leaf Lake, you eventually end up on top of some fantastic chutes on Cathedral Peak. They empty on to an open face that runs all the way down to the edge of the lake. They need a <u>lot</u> of snow because they get a lot of sun and melt out pretty easily, but they hardly ever get ridden. The main reason is that it's an incredible pain in the ass to get back to your car. There's also a great cliff band of 100'-300' lines in a bowl off the NE side of the peak.

Not until I had been up Tallac a half dozen times did I inadvertently discover a nook of the mountain that's hidden from view from most angles. Erik Wilhelm and I climbed straight up the bowl of the NE cirque one day rather than following the traditional boot pack up the ridge, and paused on top of the front mountain chutes, at the base of North Bowl. We saw two monstrous couloirs in front of us on the upper mountain that made everything else on Tallac pale.

The easier of the two, Babycham (featured on the cover of this book), starts off somewhat wide and reasonable - about 43 degrees - but steepens as it goes down and narrows into a bit of a dogleg. The choke at the bottom is 50 degrees, and it's one of the few chutes around that gets more difficult as you go. It's at least 500' of vertical until the exit, and is one of the most classic chutes of the Northern Sierra. The sister chute, Big Bird, is a hundred yards to climber's right, and is so intimidating that I watched one seasoned extreme skier climb out the top after dropping in and deciding it was too much. It's a crazy, narrow, fifty degree couloir the same length as Babycham, with a difficult entry and usually a mandatory jump turn over a six foot rock section higher up. The late Aaron "Big Bird" Martin was the only guy I knew to ever ski it. The exposure is incredible.

If you come down the skier's right side of North Bowl without veering safely off to the left like most people do, you'll find yourself on Hanging Face and the front mountain chutes. This is not a place to be if you don't know the lines. Hanging Face looks deceptively inviting, a steep buttress of snow that funnels into what looks as if it could be a chute. It's not. It's an exposed rock funnel that would be death to fall through. You have to turn right off of Hanging Face to The Central or left to S Chute, and I wouldn't advise taking those lines into either unless you've studied them ten ways to Tuesday.

The Front Chutes of Tallac, with heavy snow coverage

I did S Chute entering from the safer north side on a great powder day, and even though I had studied my reference photos of S Chute I was still taken aback by how tight and hairy it was. Sean Kelsey valiantly led the way as he had done on The Cross, going on trust that I had steered him to the right place. From the top it sure didn't look like the chute had an exit. It's board width in a few places with a hard right dogleg at the bottom, making it necessary to keep it slow and in control.

The top entry to The Central takes a bit of local knowledge to even find, and it's usually too rocky in the upper chute to do from the top. The skier's right face looks reasonable from a distance, but the funky off-camber aspect to most of it makes it far more of a challenge than people expect.

Everyone I have ever been up Tallac with has come off it feeling that everything in Tahoe they had been doing before was kind of pointless in comparison. The best thing about it is there is almost always a solid boot pack, which makes it a much faster hike than ascents which are less vertical. Best of all, though, Tallac has the terrain of about six mountains packed into it. You can never run out of new ways to descend it. The funny thing is that some Tahoe backcountry diehards have never even been up it, despite pursuing far more rigorous ascents in the Eastern (Southern) Sierra. Nothing in Tahoe can possibly measure up in their minds to the huge chutes down Highway 395. (And certainly none do for sheer size.) But of all the peaks I have seen in my travels through the Sierra, nowhere but the Sierra Buttes matches Tallac for the sheer number of extreme lines packed into such a concentrated area on one peak.

My speed up it got me the nickname "Stride Rite" from Erik Wilhelm, but Sean Kelsey shamed me by powering up in an unbelievable hour and 25 minutes. On our second lap we passed some unfortunate souls who had already been in the parking lot when we first arrived. They were still struggling haplessly toward the summit at the bottom of North Bowl. I sympathetically offered that the second lap was murder. They looked at me aghast and said "The first hike is murder!"

Desolation Wilderness

The first thing you figure out after doing a bit of backcountry in Desolation Wilderness is that you could spend your life back there and never do the same line twice. It encompasses a vast amount of terrain and at least a dozen 9000' peaks. The area is federally designated wilderness, which means no snowmobiles or any other sort of mechanical vehicle. On top of this, Desolation holds snow longer than almost anywhere else in the Northern Sierra. The only difficulty is access. In summer, Desolation is the most popular wilderness area in the US. In winter, the depths of it are used by hardly anyone.

If you want to do any Desolation backcountry beyond the front range (Tallac, Maggie's, Jake's) the first thing to do is buy the Desolation Wilderness map that the Forest Service sells. Usually you can get them at backcountry stores, but you can always try a ranger station otherwise. You'll also need to visit a ranger station to get a backcountry permit if you're planning to go out overnight.

There are two major entry points to Desolation, with a handful of others strewn about the margins. The northern entry is the Eagle Falls trailhead at Emerald Bay. This is a good way to get back to Dick's (9974') and some of the other 9000' no-names in front of it. Another way is to hike straight up Maggie's from the Bayview Trailhead and ride off the backside, which I did in the following adventure taken from my 1995 backcountry diary.

Hike up Maggie's Peaks at night with three telemarkers and a half moon. First time on cross country skis, which is awkward but I get the hang of it pretty quick. Fifty pounds of gear on my back doesn't help. The last traverse is sheer hell; tele boots filled with snow, skis getting stuck, and feet like blocks of ice. Already understanding why snowboarders don't go deep in the backcountry very often. Pitch tents in the saddle of Maggie's and get dinner cooked by midnight. Share a tiny two man tent with Karl and his dog. The dog jockeys for position the whole night and is like a ten ton rock as soon as it finds a bit of open floor. Wake up at six to a spectacular sunrise over Emerald Bay and Lake Tahoe. No one else is interested in getting up for it. So much for my hardcore image of the free heelers.

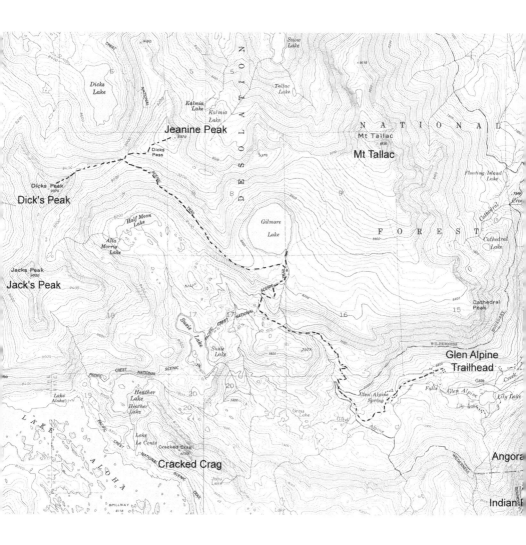

Descend the back of Maggie's into a valley north of Jeanine Peak and set up Camp #2. Above us is a big, open face with a nice gully half way down on one side. We all climb the peak, but only Geoff and Karl elect to keep going on all the way back to Dick's. At 9974', Dick's Peak is one of the three highest peaks in Desolation and the main attraction for us. It's one huge mother of a bowl that bottoms out into Dick's Lake, which is still totally frozen. The snow is deep and soft afternoon conditions and the long traverse back to camp from the lake would be a nightmare in my snowboard boots, so I opt out. Amy doesn't feel up to it either. Heavy *storm clouds are pushing in from the west, and by the time Geoff and Karl summit Dick's, they're in a total whiteout.*

Dick's Peak

I ride some lines down the face of our no name peak a few times, and then sit the storm out. The tents aren't set up yet, so I find some protection under a big rock and huddle up in my sleeping bag. It's dumping hard. The boys get back, we eat dinner early and are settled in our tents by seven, with the snow still coming down. A long night of battling with the dog for limited space. I might not have these problems if I wasn't 6'7". My tripmates have already suggested I might have life a lot easier if I telemarked, thus taking 22 pounds of board and boots off my back. Blasphemy. I scoff at them.

I'm the first one out again in the morning and glad to be out of the tent. A good freeze overnight so an easy hike up No Name. Near the top I realize how easy it would be to hike back to Dick's on the hard pack. Decide to live up to the snowboarder stereotype and totally disregard my friends, safety, and backcountry etiquette. Silly illusion that I'll be back by the time they get out of bed. Karl's dog has followed me up and won't go back to camp. Ah, well. The storm's gone, the skies are perfect Tahoe blue, and two hours later I'm on top of Dick's Peak. The top is crusty, but the whole rest of it is fresh powder all the way down to the lake. Unbelievable.

Nellie and my board, Dick's Pass

Camp has disappeared when I get back, which I worry is punishment for my transgressions, but I find their packs further down the valley. I get chastised when they return from their adventure, and Karl won't even talk to me because I'd inadvertently stolen his dog for the day. We head out along Cascade Creek, which for me turns into seven hours of hell. One tele binding is loose and rotating 180 degrees, I hopelessly flail every time I have to go downhill, and standing up again after falling becomes a major ordeal. Just before Cascade Falls I am fatigued beyond belief, barely able to continue, and have no idea where the trail is. I am despondent. Fortunately Geoff and Amy backtrack to guide me. In retrospect I fully deserved that hellish trip out.

I learn from Geoff and Amy the extent of Karl's disgust with me, that he had very intentionally left me behind on the way out. He had begrudged sharing his tent with me, as I had not been carrying it for him. He also didn't much like snowboarders, or humanity in general. My dog-napping was the last straw. It was my first lesson in why you should always consult your partners about your plans in the backcountry. Behave like I did and you'll be lucky to have anyone come back for you.

The southern entry point to Desolation is at Glen Alpine trailhead, accessed by a forest service road on the east side of Fallen Leaf Lake. This entry is closed in winter, but opens up in the spring. It's a good access point from which to hike way back to the Crystal Range peaks above Lake Aloha, as well as up to Gilmore Lake. From Gilmore you're right beneath the backside of Tallac, the Kalmia Ridge, and a short way from Jeanine's, Dick's and Jack's. Gilmore Lake is one of the larger, deeper lakes of Desolation, and it's overflowing with trout, including mackinaw. If you're there when it's unfrozen and you're doing a few nights out in Desolation, it's criminal not to have a fishing pole with you.

On a 1998 summer trip to snowboard the south face of Dick's, we camped at the lake for two nights. Both nights I had trouble getting to sleep due to a paranoid semi-conscious obsession with bears, which I normally never give any thought to. I lay frozen in terror at one point as I was convinced that one was pushing on my sleeping bag. The only animal I saw that trip was a marmot that I harassed in the name of photography out of a wood hollow, so I suspect that the weight I imagined to be leaning on me was only it coming back to get its revenge.

As far as getting back to the Crystal Range mountains, they're definitely an overnight affair. You can get in and out in one day, but it's not worth it. You'll see why in a moment, when I resort to my diary again. The other thing about the Crystals is the question of how much they're worth it at all. Some people hike in from Highway 50 to access Pyramid Peak, but you're still starting from down around 6400' or so, and you're looking at 3500' of vertical for terrain that can't remotely compare to Tallac. I know a skier, Jim Galletto, who has done the whole tour from Highway 50 through the Rubicon River Valley up to Rubicon Reservoir, climbed out of the valley and come out to Meeks Bay. For a snowboarder, that kind of tour would be only possible with a split board, but would be something worth doing if you have the backcountry skills and stamina to spend a week out there.

The Lake Aloha peaks (Pyramid Peak, Mt Price) are open faces with multitudes of rollers that get a little more technical when the snow melts out. The more interesting peaks are the ones like Red Peak and some of the others to the north of Mosquito Pass, that form the west side of the Rubicon River Valley. You can camp out along the headwaters of the river and follow the valley north, hiking up and down the walls on either side.

why bother with the Crystals, when Cracked Crag is along the way?

With the Crystals walling you in on the west and the backside of Dick's and Jack's on the east, there are one hell of a lot of two grand descents to be done there. As far as what not to do....

I recruit Erik Wilhelm for a day hike adventure even deeper into Desolation than the week before. There's still plenty of snow in the Crystal Range overlooking Lake Aloha. It's three and a half hours back to Lake Aloha, but a beautiful hike past a lot of high mountain lakes. We leave our gear at the north end of Aloha and climb up Mosquito Pass, then up the ridge line to the snowfield under Mount Price.

Erik attempts to launch over a rock, doesn't quite clear it, and nearly cracks his head open when he catches his nose and does a full cartwheel over the rock. An inauspicious debut. We traverse across the snowfield in search of good terrain, with the massive granite walls of Mt Price towering above us. The sheer cliffs, a hundred feet high in places, are an unbelievable mix of colors and textures. By the time we decide to head back down to the lake it's five o'clock. The descent is a tricky negotiation of steep, dead-end chutes, where we have to unstrap and climb our way down to the next patch of snow again and again. I get the bright idea of taking a shortcut across Lake Aloha, thus saving us the time of walking all the way around it to our stuff. Erik is skeptical. The idea is based on linking all the rock islands together across the lake. From up above they looked like they formed a chain all the way across.

Erik Wilhelm, wondering why he's following a lunatic

We get three quarters of the way to the other side, and find a channel too wide to jump across. Rather than being a placid lake on the north side, Aloha is more a series of rock pools of different elevations. The water flows off toward the falls at the south end, and there was a strong current flowing through the channel. I take off my boots and wade across without too much trouble, and then Erik goes for it. Midway, he begins to lose his footing and a look of pure panic crosses his face. He looks sure that he's going under. With a desperate lunge, he launches himself at the rock on the other side and barely makes it. We climb up on top of this rock outcropping, and see that the chain has ended. The only way to the next series of rocks is to swim.

Insanely enough, I'm willing to. I have trouble admitting defeat. It's all so close. Erik will have nothing to do with my idiotic notions, and convinces me that we should backtrack and walk around the lake. Probably a good thing. Don't want to add pneumonia to the list of things that have resulted from my trips. Not prudent. Don't want to go there. On the way back across the channel we hurl our boards at the other side, smashing them into the rocks. A bad sign that we've given up caring already.

By the time we reach the rim of the lake and start hiking around, it gets dark. This is not good. We were supposed to get back to the car by dark. The rim of the lake is a jumble of huge boulders and is very slow hiking. I am very unhappy. Erik is very unhappy. Expletives echo through the darkness whenever one of us stumbles. Halfway back to the north end where our gear is, the full moon rises. This makes me feel better, letting myself accept that we're not going to get out for a long time and we have the moon to guide us. We finally reach our gear around eight o'clock, rest, and forge onward.

Shadows cover parts of the trail, and we stumble a fair bit on the hike out. The expletives continue. Our shoulders are screaming with soreness. Our bodies are wrecked. We lose the trail at times. Because both of us are putting up a front of stoic endurance, neither knows how miserable the other actually is. This is good. It keeps us going. We reach the car at eleven o'clock, fourteen hours, fifteen miles, and four thousand feet of vertical climbing from when we began. It is agreed that we should reconsider our definition of day hike in the future.

Though it involves a brutal climb to do with a lot of gear on, my favorite way to access the Desolation backcountry now is via Tallac. It's by far the quickest way to gain a huge amount of vertical, and climbing a bootpack with a load is a hell of a lot easier than hiking many miles over uneven terrain. Once you're on the backside of Tallac, the Kalmia Ridge is right beneath you with some beautiful cornice drops and chutes. This whole cirque between Tallac and Jeanine Peak is a wonderland of steeps. Most of the runs are only 1000' shots, but that means you can do more of them. Once you're up this high, everything is rapid access by hiking the ridges. It's not far on Kalmia Ridge to Jeanine Peak, and behind it to Dick's Pass. The bonus is that when you ride out at the end of a trip you get the Tallac descent as your final memory. Which is much more sweet than Cascade Creek, trust me.

Jeanine Peak with Dick's behind it and the cliffs above Tallac Lake in the foreground

More great steeps terrain in Desolation can be found behind Fallen Leaf Lake on the climber's left side of the valley that the Glen Alpine Trail runs through, from Angora Peak (8588') to Indian Rock (8620') to Cracked Crag (8720'). I was scouting back there one day to find a chute that was visible from Tallac, and I thought I found it by Indian Rock. This rock face is a dramatic 800' cliff that is one of the longest, sheer drops around Tahoe, and there are big couloirs running down either side. Once I was finished shooting reference photos, I grabbed my board and hiked up Angora Peak to do one of its gully lines for some late spring fun. When I got up on Angora, one of my irrational impulses came over me and I decided I wanted to do what I came to call Fallen Angel Chute, on skier's right of Indian Rock. To summarize the experience, the snow was bad, my choices were bad, and I came so close to dying it still scares me.

Desolation lives up to its name. You're generally a long way from help, and you have to exercise a lot of wisdom in what you do. Keep this foremost in your mind when you get a wild hair in Desolation.

The next time I hiked to the top of Angora, I rode from the top of the peak to the gully that I had eyed up in the first place. The top 800' is a great steep tree run, and you veer to the left to enter the gully for the next 1200'. The gully faces north toward Cathedral Peak and Tallac, and drops you very close to the trail and the parking area. Entering the gully is the only trick, because it's quite steep for the top hundred feet and requires the navigation of some mini-chutes before you make it into the wide, playful part. In powder it's an effortless dream, though it is a classic avalanche gully and needs to be respected as such. Off the north face there is a fantastic rock garden full of chutes and drops, and an adjacent chute to Fallen Angel that's a mellower pitch. If you drop straight down from the saddle you enter this chute, whereas you start from the top of Indian Rock to access Fallen Angel. This whole face does require a lot of snow to fill in properly, though, and on some years none of these lines are do-able.

I got the name for the chute from mixing a bit of literature – Kerouac's "Desolation Angels" – with the nearby lake – Fallen Leaf – and adding my own misfortune to the brew. Only recently I discovered Mark Twain could have easily been the inspiration for my flight of fancy. He had an amusing rant against the name "Tahoe" at one point, a name he apparently hated, though he loved the lake deeply.

"Of course Indian names are more fitting than any others for our beautiful lakes and rivers, which knew their race ages ago, perhaps, in the morning of creation, but let us have none so repulsive to the ear as "Tahoe" for the beautiful relic of fairy-land forgotten and left asleep in the snowy Sierras when the little elves fled from their ancient haunts and quitted the earth. They say it means 'Fallen Leaf' - well suppose it meant fallen devil or fallen angel, would that render its hideous, discordant syllables more endurable? Not if I know myself. I yearn for the scalp of the soft-shell crab - be he injun or white man - who conceived of that spoony, slobbering, summer-complaint of a name."

On the skier's left side of Indian Rock is Halls of the Gods, a dramatic 600' couloir that leaps out at you when you look south from Tallac. Dan Hunt was the first snowboarder to ride this chute back in 1992, and it hasn't been ridden by many snowboarders since. Grant Barta and some other skiers have done it, but it's definitely one of the hidden jewels of the Northern Sierra. Halls is pretty straightforward, 45 degrees up top, and lined by high rock walls. There are at least three different entry halls you can take for the first 200', depending on how difficult you want to make it. The skier's right line is the narrowest and most challenging, though the center line is a smoother and faster one. The right entry may be over 45 degrees until you come through the choke into the main chute, and it's not always filled in enough to do. No matter which entry you take, it's definitely not a chute you want to screw up at the top.

l to r: north face of Angora Peak, Fallen Angel Chute, Indian Rock, Halls of the Gods

Off the top of the 8720' peak just fifty yards up the ridge to skier's left is Mini Hall, about half the length and a few degrees less steep. It's a good backup plan for anyone not up to holding it together for the length of Halls of the Gods, and it's still a great chute.

Dave Frissyn, Halls of the Gods

On the other side of Indian Rock, Fallen Angel Chute is the longest of all of them, coming in more towards 800' of vertical in length. You ride off the east side of Indian Rock down an ever-steepening face, which funnels tightly into the choke of the chute. This is a place you really don't want to make a mistake. I did. There is nothing more horrifying than beginning an out of control slide above the choke, and knowing you're going to pinball off of rocks all the way down, with death the guaranteed outcome. This is why an ice ax is a must for doing this kind of chute when you're unsure about the snow and/or your own skill. (My friend Jason Schutz used two in his early years of doing frozen chutes in Chamonix.) I didn't have one, but was saved by the freak chance of my board catching in a cleft after my body had only absorbed one bounce off the walls. Unless there's a good amount of coverage, a rock dries out in the choke and forces a down-climb or mandatory air. Below this point the pitch mellows out some and it's not too bad the rest of the way.

Indian Rock is another winter hike for the truly dedicated, because there's no road access for miles in any direction. The quickest way is to climb the backside of Indian Rock, from Angora Lakes, but it's a long trek in from one of the South Lake neighborhoods just to get to the lakes. In addition, you don't really want to do any of these chutes unless you've looked at them from in front before. Many years Fallen Angel doesn't ever fill in enough to do. Halls is a little more dependable, but it takes a lot of snow to fill in as well. Problem is, the road into Fallen Leaf Lake is closed back near Hwy 89, forcing a long cross-country trip to get back to the Glen Alpine Trailhead and scout the frontside. Split boards or skis are the call, and camping for a few nights makes the most sense so you can take full advantage of the wealth of terrain. The best way to scout is during a trip up Tallac, which gives you a panoramic view of all the lines. You can also ride down from Tallac off the west face of Cathedral Peak to get there, which has some epic chute lines of its own.

Finally, toward the northern end of Desolation there are some crazy steep lines off of Crag Peak and an un-named one I call 9310', which you stare straight back at when you're atop Jake's. The imposing NE face of Crag Peak, a massive dihedral, develops under the right conditions into an infamous mixed rock and ice mountaineering route. These peaks are just to the north of Phipp's Peak and descend into a deep valley behind Stony Ridge. The best way to access them is via Phipp's by hiking up the Eagle

Falls trailhead. After the descent to Stony Ridge Lake, you can hike up the backside of Jake's and tack on one of the descents of it for an epic double peak day. This is no day hike for the timid, though, and has remained mostly the province of telemarkers. Between avalanche danger, uncertainty over how frozen the lakes are, and the long distance and many thousands of vertical feet of hiking involved, any foray back to these peaks must involve some serious thought and planning.

9310' to Crag Peak, viewed from Jake's

Freel Peak/Job's Sister/Job's Peak

The triumvirate of ten granders that loom over the south shore of Lake Tahoe are a question mark to most, and my knowledge of them is still entirely second hand. Access is difficult, the peaks are regularly blasted by hurricane force winds, and much of the terrain isn't very interesting. Looking south toward them, Freel Peak (10,881') is the largest and westernmost one. The terrain off of all sides is fairly mellow, though there is a small hidden cirque on the south side that has some short, steep lines.

Adjacent to Freel is Job's Sister (10,823') which has some very steep chutes and north face pitches leading down to Star Lake, which sits at just over 9000'. This is some of the most challenging terrain on the upper sections of the Freel/Job's plateau. I've had friends who hiked up the forest roads from South Lake Tahoe to Star Lake, camped and then ascended, but it was an agonizingly long and slow spring ascent. I also know the Barta brothers and Erik Wilhelm have reached it by snowmobile from Luther Pass.

Further to the east is Job's Peak (10,633'), and falling off its northern and eastern faces are some of the most majestic winter descents you can do in the Northern Sierra. Whereas everything on the Tahoe basin side of this plateau meanders downhill slowly, with little to interest the backcountry steeps seeker, the Carson Valley side of these mountains is a huge drop of over 5000' of vertical to the valley floor. Job's Peak rolls slowly off to a sub-peak at 9800', and then the next 4000' is an unrelentingly steep gully line down the east face. Low snow levels are needed for this descent, because it doesn't flatten out until about the 5000' elevation level. Also, this side of the range traditionally gets the least snow. Imagine, though, when the snow is right for it: 5600' of vertical! Throw that in the face of the next jaded person who belittles everything in the Northern Sierra for being too small. I saw it ready to go in the mega-winters of '98/'99 and '92/'93. A skier friend of mine did it in March 2000, though he had to do a bit of bushwhacking to get out. On the north face of Job's Peak are some huge chutes that drop into Job's Canyon, but after the first two thousand feet of steeps, the long descent from there is down mellow canyon floor.

Closer to Heavenly Ski Area, on the north side of Job's Canyon, there's a 9700' peak that has even better terrain as far as cliffs and rocks.

It lies just to the east of Star Lake, which is the most centrally located and sheltered camping spot for multi-day trips. This peak has a mere 3700' of steeps before it mellows out. Off the south face of Job's Peak, dropping into Fay Canyon, there are countless more 4000'+ monster lines. For huge, untapped terrain in the Tahoe area, this is definitely where it's at.

I've always thought of coming in from the backside via Luther Pass as the best approach for the east face descents, but that's six miles of trekking to save yourself 2000' of vertical and you have to set a shuttle car down in the Carson Valley fifteen miles away.

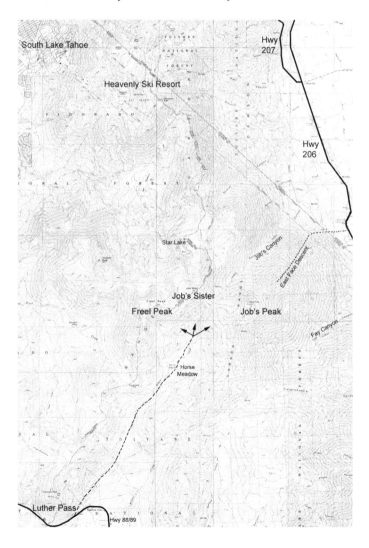

Erik Wilhelm, Job's Sister   (photo: Grant Barta)

For day trips to the east faces, I think climbing straight up the beasts might be the way to do it. That way you get a better sense of snow conditions, because any slide you set off on one of these faces is going to turn into a juggernaut. I've never been able to find any access off of Hwy 206 to get you closer to the base of these peaks, though maps do show some sort of track that loops from 206 up to the base of Job's Canyon and back. Without the rare event of a winter with some heavy snows down to 5000', though, the best descents just don't happen.

Photos on following pages:

Mt Rose

Aside from Donner Summit, the peaks around Mt Rose are home to the most heavily populated backcountry in the Northern Sierra. Part of this is its proximity to Reno, and another major factor is the convenience of pass hiking. The pass atop Mt Rose Highway tops out at 8900', which is higher than many of Tahoe's mountains, and it's the highest pass that's open year-round in the Sierra. Whenever it rains at lake level - which those familiar with many seasons of Sierra cement know that it often does - you can depend on it to be snowing up on the Rose peaks. The highest of the peaks, Mt Rose (10,776'), doesn't have much to offer because most of it is blasted regularly by such howling winds that snow cannot stick to its face.

Jeff Krebill, Tamarack Peak

Most people hike from the top of the pass or just a bit to either side, and don't go more than a half mile from the road. On the lake side, in Mt Rose Meadows, kickers spring up everywhere that a transition can be found. If you're only looking for kickers and enjoy the sounds of snow-mobiles whining, then the meadows is the place. Off the top of the pass you can hike the east-west ridge, and within twenty minutes of hiking you'll find a nice set of cornices on the Reno side. The ridge continues to ascend above an open bowl, with another set of bigger cornices. It then winds to the north up to Tamarack Peak, with a steep east face bowl scattered with trees. This is actually a pretty fun descent, though most snowboarders stop before they get this far. It runs for about 800' of vertical down to the Hourglass kickers, which are the main focus of most photo and film crews who come here.

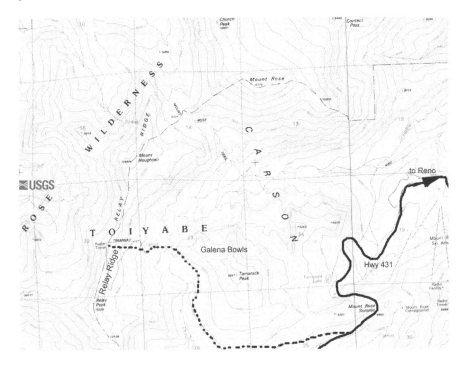

Further back, the ridge climbs very slightly for a few hundred yards to the west, which puts you on top of Galena Bowls, a set of north-facing bowls with about a 1200' vertical drop. These bowls hold powder for a long time and are great descents, but leave you in Galena Creek at the bottom of a canyon that you have to hike back out of. There are some steeper rock and chute lines on the opposite side of the canyon, so you might as well do them, too, if you're going to go to the canyon floor. Otherwise you have to start traversing to skier's right and climb over a small ridge back if you want to come back out on the front face and get back to your car again on Mt Rose Highway. Most people park on the side of the road about a third of a mile down from the top of the pass on the Reno side, and hike straight to Tamarack Peak and the Galena Bowls from there. It's much quicker than starting from the ridge on top of the pass.

Tom Wayes, Galena Bowls

Yet farther back from Galena Bowls is a north-south ridge called Relay Ridge, framed at one end by Relay Peak (10,338') and Mt Houghton (10,490') at the other. Midway along it you'll see a prominent group of radio towers. The east bowl of Relay Peak has a steep 1000' face descent through a choke of rocks, and one beautiful, long descent off the south ridge back toward the meadows. Off the west side of Relay Peak are some challenging chutes and steeps, but you have to climb back up the ridge to ride out. Snowmobilers and film crews come back to Relay Ridge quite a bit, but the wilderness boundary is on top of the ridge. If you see any cross to the west side, let them know. Most of them simply aren't familiar with the boundaries, and there aren't any signs.

A spine breaks off from Relay Peak and extends to the west, connecting to a sub-peak littered with beautiful chute lines. They make your mouth water they seem so close and inviting, but they're a deceptively long distance away yet. One day when I was in Florida, I got a call from Dave Frissyn announcing that he was standing on top of them. He had gone on a split board solo mission, and I was the only person he knew who would fully appreciate and envy where he was. Unless you have a split-board system or get an early start, this area is a little far for day hikes. If you want to spend a night, though, it opens up all kinds of possibilities. Backcountry diary 1999:

After three hours, reach the tramway building beneath Relay Ridge. Been day tripping too long, forty pound packs don't feel so good. Probably why I don't camp more. Chris is exhausted. No wonder, he's a sea-level boy who just got a massive workout at nine to ten grand. Find a tree shelter, and dig out a three foot deep pit to set the tent down in. Chris teaches me a few tricks about snow camping, such as filling tent bags and carry sacks with snow, tying anchor lines to them and burying them another two feet under. Good things to know. When accommodations for the night are secured, we hike to the radio towers on top of the ridge and have a look around. The chutes and spines just to the west look insane, and I can't wait for the next morning to do them. We do a powder run back toward the camp, and hike up to do another. Chris lands bad off a small air at the bottom of the run, and worries he has hurt his knee. We decide to see how it is in the morning.

Chris Roddick, before things went wrong

Dinner is some awful salty noodle mush that we cook badly. A storm passes through overnight, and it's eerie to listen to fifty mile per hour gusts howling over the tops of the trees. Our shelter proves to be bombproof, thanks to Chris, and we sleep okay. When we wake up in the morning, Chris declares he can't walk. His knee is swollen up double size. I go out for a quick powder run before we make our final decision, but it looks like we're headed out. He gets to the point where he can move, but not very well. I lash together both our snowboards, pile both our packs on top of them, and tie the makeshift sled behind me with some string. Chris limps behind on his snowshoes, using his poles to support most of his weight.

sunrise over our camp spot under Relay Ridge

The sled isn't bad to tow, but slides off the trail whenever the slope is off camber. After a few hours of hiking, with the road only a mile and a half away, some snowmobilers pass by and I get them to take Chris out with them. Determined that this is good for my character, I decline the offer for them to take me as well. Bright choice. Ten minutes later the sled slides off the trail, the tow string breaks, and it rockets down the hill until it partially decimates a small pine and comes to a stop. I spend *another twenty minutes trying to jam everything back together into a towable unit, and keep going. When I reach the downhill into the meadow, I'm worried that if I try to ride the sled down on my belly I'll pick up an enormous amount of speed and spectacularly crash into some tree or innocent sledding family down below. Bit by bit I work my way down the hill, trying to keep the sled from getting away from me. It falls apart again. I'm getting a bit pissed off by now. After another hour of struggling, I finally get the damn thing out to the road.*

Just at the point all should be relief and happiness, I discover that I've lost my keys. We search everything for an hour until I figure out they must have fallen out of my jacket back around camp or on the way out. I can't find a phone anywhere around the summit to use, and eventually we find a nice pair of young hikers who are passing by my house on their way home. The car can wait. I get home and figure out I have no spare key.

On Monday I go up with Chris to break in to my locked car on top of the summit. Chris gets a little overzealous and shatters the window. I don't even care. We get the passenger door lock out with the key code on it, and the next morning I drive to Reno to get a new key made. New key, back to the summit, only to discover my car has been towed. Spend rest of the day trying to figure where it was towed to, before finding out it's been taken all the way out to Sparks. Add on towing charge of $133, and all the ugly repercussions of this trip are put to rest. The simple pleasures of the backcountry...

For years I looked wistfully at the face of Rose Knob Peak (9710'), one of the closest of the Rose peaks to the lake. It actually had a long descent to it, which was what interested me. Occasionally I saw tracks on it, but by and large not a lot of people did it. I didn't know the best access to it, and it always seemed just a bit too far back to bother with. Every time I tried to interest someone they pointed out the distance. It was only in the winter of 1998 that I finally figured out the lay of the land, and found the short way up. Strangely enough, and independent of my interest, suddenly everyone I talked to had just been up there, was going up there, and sang the praises of the place. So much for discovery. Still, the popularity was mainly among people I knew, and skiers at that. The bulk of the mountain was still untapped.

Figuring out the incredible maze of neighborhood roads on the west side of Mount Rose Highway (431) was half the effort. I finally settled on two parking areas and routes. The parking is roadside parking and legal, but don't park in the way of the snow plows. If you turn left opposite the Incline Mountain Golf Course, immediately turn right on Jennifer, and proceed all the way to a cul-de-sac at the end, you'll be at the bottom of the east face runs.

Heather Stoneman

Jeff Krebill

Once atop Rose Knob Peak there are a lot of different ways to go. Just below the summit, there's a cornice line along the east side of the ridge that's okay for 10-15' drops. Taking the main bowl off the peak is carving at its best, but you have to watch you don't end up in the creek canyon, like I once did on a spring day. If you bear high right before you hit the canyon you'll be fine, but most of the descent from there is a dull high traverse unless you regain the top of the ridge. Alternately you can go far left, but you'll eventually have to unstrap and cross the creek. A warning about this face: It's another classic avalanche path, and back around 1982 it let go a tremendous slide that piled up 60 feet of snow at the bottom.

My favorite descent path is the lake side of the east-west ridge you climbed up. There are windlips, rock drops, and a lot of wide open carving all the way down. The key is to stay high on the ridge until you hit the rock outcroppings, and then you can drop to your right into the gully from there. The last - and possibly best - face of Rose Knob Peak is the SW back bowl, wrapping around to Rose Knob (9600'). The view of the lake is incredible. There are cornices, vertical banks to slash, rock outcroppings... it's a great playland. You just have to be careful you know your way in and out from here.

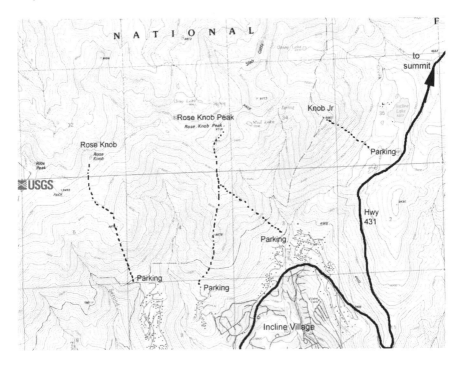

To get there, you take the same turn off of Mount Rose Highway and right on to Jennifer that you would going to the other parking, but then turn left on Geraldine, right on Randall, and just keep following roads in the uphill direction until the top, where you turn right on Alison and go to the end. There's a National Forest trailhead near a water tower.

Yet one more starting point gets you slightly higher, to about 7700' elevation. It's at the top of one of mine and Dave Frissyn's favorite longboard skate runs. Turning left on Barbara going up Mount Rose Highway, you turn left on Jennifer this time and right where it meets Tyner Way. Follow Tyner as far as you can to the top and seek out a parking spot that seems low key. This puts you on climber's left of the creek that drains from between Rose Knob Peak and Rose Knob, giving you the same access to the back bowl of Rose Knob Peak. It puts you closer to Rose

Knob and Rifle Peak, and on the north side of Rifle Peak there are some hidden chute lines that are only visible from Relay Ridge.

Between the maze of neighborhoods and maze of peaks, this is an extremely confusing area. For years I was calling the wrong peaks Rose Knob and Rose Knob Peak (whoever thought up these inanely similar names was no doubt equally confused). Every time I recognized my mistake, I'd wrongly assign the names to another pair of peaks. I went through three or four configurations before getting them right. Part of the problem is that there are a couple of nearly-as-high or higher adjacent peaks which are unnamed.

the author, briefly carefree about which way the car is   (photo: James Lichtenstein)

Though I've had some minor routefinding problems on my descents of the Knob family, I haven't experienced nearly the problems which others have had from west of Rose Knob, between Rifle Peak and Mt

Baldy. There are no high neighborhoods to come out in, and you quickly run into thick forest and lose your way. I recommend learning the Rose Knob Peak routes first and coming back out that way even if you go all the way back to Rifle Peak. Too many people have gotten lost back here, and Search and Rescue is strapped enough as it is.

During one of my first seasons in Tahoe, a nordic skier in Mt Rose Meadows disappeared without a trace, not to be found until the spring thaw. Following that, someone decided he wanted to see how the person could have gotten lost up there, and guess what? He never came back. I'm not one to over-promote technology, but until you know this area like the back of your hand, a cell phone and a handheld GPS are damn fine company to have on a trip.

Tom Wayes

Up Mt Rose Highway past the 8000' elevation marker, you drive right beside a nameless peak I call Knob Junior (9561'). There's a parking area on the west side of the road to start hiking from. The ascent is quick and steep, and there's limited choice in descents. The SE face is probably the best single shot, a very steep run of about 1600' of vertical. It has innumerable drifts you can air, like a park radically tilted. Coverage is the only problem, because the winds blast this face and the sun bakes it as well. There's also a south face route, which flattens out briefly on a bench, and then descends again down to the creek canyon coming off of Rose Knob. If you shuttle a car, this is a healthy dose of vertical (2200'). On the east side of the peak, not far from the road, is a small chute/cliff area with some good lines to be had that no one ever seems to do.

east face of Knob Jr

Down the Reno side of the pass, the Slide Chutes come into play once Mt Rose Ski Area has closed for the season (around the end of April). These are an impressively steep set of chutes and gullies which would make the ski area a whole different place if they were ever open to lift-accessed riding. They cover almost the entire north face of Slide Mountain, and are popular because they can be shuttled by hiking from the top of the pass over to them and ending up down on the road.

Alpine Meadows/Squaw Valley

The backcountry immediately adjacent to the resorts of Alpine Meadows and Squaw Valley is often overlooked. If it isn't something accessible without too much hiking from the resort boundaries, lift junkies ignore it, and because it's so close to the bustle, so do most of the backcountry crowd. Alpine Meadows is fairly liberal with its boundary policy, and they try to open the out-of-bounds traverses fairly quickly after storms. Most of Alpine's best terrain is on the fringes - Munchkin Chutes, Beaver and Estelle Bowl, Cartoonland, the Grouse Rock to Twin Peaks ridge - and this terrain involves some hiking. (The Grouse-to-Twin ridge is part of Ward Valley, and can be found in that section.) In addition, most of it is not avalanche controlled so it's your job to be responsible when you head out of bounds.

Squaw Valley, on the other hand, has the most rigid and actively enforced boundary policies around, and there are no backcountry gates. Everything outside the ski area is one hundred percent closed all the time to backcountry access. Further complicating things is the large parcel of private property between Alpine and Squaw that's owned by Troy Caldwell. He used to be more accommodating about letting people hike on his property but liability issues have forced him to put up closed signs. The beautiful cliff area known as White Wolf is now off limits to all but a few select film crews. Though illegal backside runs off of KT-22 have gotten to be all too common in recent years, the tragedy in February 2001 of two young ski racers killed in an avalanche is a reminder of just how dangerous this terrain is. Even where backcountry access from resorts is legal, too many people approach it without the caution required: You should approach backcountry terrain with the same mindset coming off a lift as you would five miles deep in completely foreign terrain.

One of the most obvious backcountry - or frontcountry - attractions in the Alpine Meadows area is a face that has many names. Avy Chutes, A Chutes, Highway Patrol Chutes - whatever you want to call them, they're not even chutes, really, more like funnels through a somewhat ill-defined mass of giant rock outcroppings and trees. Just across Highway 89 from Alpine Meadows Road, this terrain takes a good snow year to fill in. Even when it does fill in, the sun exposure melts it out very quickly, so opportunities are limited.

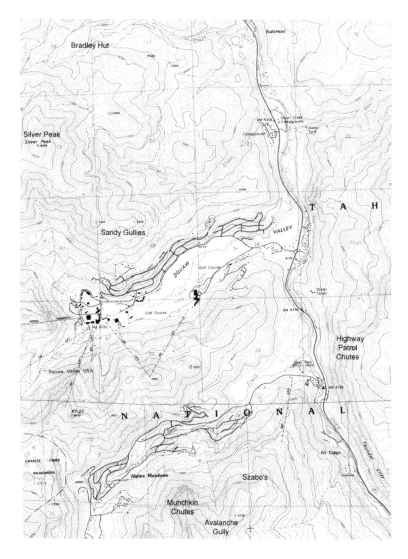

A lot of caution should be exercised here in the fresh powder of winter. If you get caught in a slide, chances are that you'll be deposited out in the road. (Thus the Highway Patrol will be digging you out.) You can't outrun the slides either, because the lines get steeper the farther down you go. While the steeps are about 800' of vertical, above them is another 600' of mellower open terrain that's a good prelude to dropping the main part. You're only at 7600' on top, but you can see south to Rubicon, back to Twin Peaks, Alpine, Squaw, Silver, Tinker's - it's not a bad view.

Scott Grevious, Highway Patrol Chutes

Even in the worst conditions for hiking - sinking knee to waist deep and setting the bootpack - it takes no more than an hour to gain the top of the steeps. It's an easy one to knock off when you only have time for a quickie or you just want to go do a sunset run.

Driving up Alpine Meadows Road almost all the way to the resort, you'll see an extremely steep exposure on your left. These are the Munchkin Chutes. They contain some of the best technical lines at the north end of the lake, and with a northern exposure they hold their snow well into the summer. Looking at them climber's left to right takes you from heart-stopping to easiest. The most difficult one is called Chad's Choice after Chad Bateman, who died there attempting to be the first to ski it on March 15, 1992. After four or five turns on the hanging face, the slope avalanched, sending him over the cliff below. He hit rock when landing, and slid another 800 feet down the slope into the forest.

Very few people since have been willing to try the line, though it has been successfully skied on rare occasions. You have to hug the skier's right side of the hanging face and sneak into the lower half of the chute midway down, or you're stuck with a mandatory forty to hundred foot air. With even the slightest question about snow conditions, it's like playing Russian Roulette. Of the few that have ventured over here, most have opted for the chute entry lower down and to the right of the hanging face, which itself is one of the most difficult chutes around Tahoe. While the tight part of the chute is only about 100 feet long, it is board width in the middle and easily 50 degrees.

Next over is M1, a steep face funneling into a tight exit that usually involves a mandatory air. From afar, it looks pretty reasonable, but it's deceptively steep and the choke can be intimidating. I passed on it my first time out when it was untracked, and more recently one of my friends- an old hand at Alpine Meadows – climbed back out from above the choke after deciding she wasn't up to doing it alone that day. In a good snow year it can be no more than a funnel, but with less snow it becomes a mandatory air though it. Beside it is M2, which is basically a rock-walled gully run with beautiful banks to surf at high speed. M3 isn't even a chute, just an open face run off the NW corner of the ridge.

In the other direction, out toward Hwy 89, is a set of steep tree runs called Szabo's, which is fun to do on a heavy powder day where the avalanche danger is too high elsewhere. Between the backside of the

Munchkin Chutes and Szabo's is Avalanche Gully, a favorite deep powder stash of locals. There are some great steeps lines down into the gully from either side, with a number of mini-chutes and cliff drops. Beware the huge cornices at the top of the gully, though, and remember that it's called Avalanche Gully for a reason.

Munchkin Chutes, in a heavy snow year

On the north side of Alpine Meadows Road - below the backside of Squaw's KT22 - is the White Wolf area. Access here has been closed for some time now by Troy Caldwell, the owner of the property, and will likely remain so. The ridge starts at the Alpine Meadows boundary area called Cartoonland and runs for about a mile to the north before bending around west and petering out at Five Lakes. There used to be a back-country hut at Five Lakes run by the Sierra Club, but by 1996 it was in a state of disrepair, compounded by a tree falling through it. The hut was demolished and the new Bradley Hut has been relocated to the north in the Pole Creek drainage of Silver Peak. Technically, a large section of the northern cliffs of White Wolf is Granite Chief Wilderness, but you almost invariably trespass on Caldwell's property coming or going to it. I came down with some friends through his backyard once, thinking at the time his house was some sort of Alpine Meadows maintenance facility, and he was surprisingly polite about the incursion. He's a good guy who's just trying to avoid liability issues, so respect his posted boundaries.

Carsten Bahnson, Cartoonland

Moving over to Squaw Valley and heading up Squaw Valley Rd, there's some good terrain to be had in the NW corner of the valley. The elevation is 600' lower than it is at the base of Alpine Meadows Ski Area, so the snow doesn't tend to be as good in winter. A popular short hike for locals is straight up behind the Olympic Village Inn, which has fun cornices and windlips up top. Just to the east of here above Sandy Way are the Sandy Gullies, which are a nice set of steep, 800' gully lines with some beautiful windlips. There is no public parking along Sandy, though, and homeowners get very irate at anyone that parks illegally. From Olympic Village Inn - known to locals as just OVI - you can also head up Shirley Canyon, with all kinds of small cliff terrain and rollers on the north side. The climber's left part is Squaw property. Farther to the north is Silver Peak (8424'), best reached by hiking up a gully to a saddle due north of OVI. The east face of Silver has an open bowl for some 600' of vertical and then becomes a tree run out to Hwy 89. In the Pole Creek drainage, on the upper part of this descent, is the Bradley Hut. On the south face of Silver there are usually windlips along the ridge that are fun to slash while descending toward OVI.

Erik Wilhelm, gully slash

North on the Pacific Crest from Silver Peak is a large, cliff-laden ridge that has some beautiful, east-facing steeps lines when the snow fills in enough. This ridge is halfway between Silver Peak and Tinker's Knob, and is probably one of the most rarely skied faces of quality steeps in this area. Unless you're doing a crest tour and emptying out at Squaw or Sugar Bowl, though, it's not a practical hike. Like Silver Peak, most of the descent toward Highway 89 is through thick trees and relatively flat terrain.

Much of Granite Chief Wilderness is comprised of the valley on the west side of Alpine Meadows and Squaw Valley, where the Middle Fork of the American River begins. The peaks diminish heading west toward the foothills, and even for the ambitious hiker there's little to search out in this area in terms of peak descents or steep terrain. One of the few exceptions is the small cirque called Sunken Meadow at the south edge of the wilderness boundary, behind Twin Peaks and accessible from Blackwood Canyon.

elastic man Erik Wilhelm, crail grab with a pack on

Donner Summit

ASI/Billy Mack

Had the Donner Party been snowboarders or freeskiers....well, they would have eaten each other a lot quicker. The pass area that holds such a memorable place in American legend for its grisly tales of cannibalism and survival also happens to be one of the great playlands of snowboard and ski greats. For years I ignored it, reasoning that it was overplayed. As a photographer, though, I learned people didn't want to hike very far for photo shoots. Because there's so much good, accessible terrain there, I finally made my peace with the place and discovered the pleasures of it.

The majority of Tahoe backcountry shots in magazines have been from this area, despite few of the lines being longer than 300'. Any video you've seen featuring Tahoe backcountry has likely included a lot of Donner footage. Again, this is more what you'd call frontcountry, because many of the cliff drops and chutes are within a couple hundred yards of the road. A prominent band of cliffs sits just behind the Alpine Skills International headquarters at the top of the pass – recently joined by the Sugar Bowl Academy - and more lie directly across the street. The whole area coming down from the north face of Mt Judah through the cliffs to here is commonly known and referred to as "ASI". (My usage of the term ASI is in this context and doesn't relate to the facility, which is one of the best backcountry training centers in the United States.)

The best and worst thing to happen to the ASI region was the addition of the Mt Judah lift at Sugar Bowl in 1996. As far as the terrain the Judah lift opened up for Sugar Bowl, it was relatively pointless. It's pretty much a lift for the snowboard park. The advantage for backcountry enthusiasts is that it effectively created a lift for ASI and the east bowl faces of Judah. Though Sugar Bowl's boundary policies have always been some of the most liberal around Tahoe, the policy toward out of bounds into ASI has been wide open. Jim Zellers is the person who is much to thank for this, because he and other backcountry enthusiasts encouraged the Forest Service to allow the new lift only with the stipulation it must

Jaison LeRoy, ASI   Shea Paxson, ASI

have a backcountry gate.

The ASI cliffs had long been an accident waiting to happen when Burton team rider Jamil Khan died there in early 1998. After Jamil's unfortunate death, I've seen dozens of people do roughly the same thing as he did, with much less of an idea what they were doing. If you don't know the ASI cliffs well and you ride down from the Judah lift, you end up on top of the cliffs with no idea where you are. I've seen so many people do this; walk out to the edge and peer over to see where they're at, and then hike back up and traverse around to the mellowest way down. Any one of them could have broken off a cornice and fallen to serious injury or death.

I was with a group of friends at Sugar Bowl the day Jamil died, and we were minutes from heading up Judah to ride down through Poop Chute - at the base of which Jamil got buried - when we heard about the avalanche. We postponed our lap until I drove over to ASI and found out what had happened, and discovered the area closed. I've found in the time since that so many stories went around about the accident that very few people accurately know the details. Jamil was approaching the highest part of the cliff band that forms the rider's left wall of Poop Chute. When Jamil was walking out to check his line, still well back from the edge, an

the cliff area at Donner Summit the day Jamil Khan died – you can see where the cornice broke off in the upper right and the fracture line of the avalanche in the lower left

enormous section of cornice broke out from under him. He fell at least eighty feet with the cornice, which set off a slide upon impact. The slide went less than a hundred yards down into the flat, but combined with the cornice rubble was substantial enough to bury him four feet under. Because he wasn't wearing an avalanche transceiver, it took rescuers too long to find him. (From what I understand, he had one but it was either in his pack nearby or down in his car.) At that point he had a weak pulse but died on the way to the hospital.

I was especially disturbed by the accident, because it was a hard reminder that what you think of as a playground can also be a lurking deathtrap. The same would have happened to anyone who ventured out on that cornice that day, regardless of whether they had any business there or not. Countless people over the years had hucked those same cliffs in deeper, fresh snow without incident, and even more had wandered out onto them not knowing where they were, but cornices are unstable by their nature. If something of a freak accident, it was long overdue.

While I had been ambivalent to that point about the need for an avalanche transceiver in Tahoe backcountry, utilizing common sense in one's place, Jamil's death committed me to wearing one a transceiver one hundred percent of the time. Tahoe may be stable compared to elsewhere, but there are a lot of different ways to get buried and they generally happen when you least expect it. To my ongoing horror, I've found that nothing has changed up there in people's awareness. On every bluebird powder day there are dozens of people coming down from the Judah chair or hiking up, and few know the place at all. Even half the pros and film crews who shoot there don't know where the cornice is that broke off. A year after Jamil's death, it was overhanging really badly again by April, heavily loaded by new snow, and there were people traipsing over it left and right. Many people still think Jamil was riding down Poop Chute and it slid, because he ended up in the same place that he would have if that had been the case.

Because the ASI area is so popular and it's so easy to end up where you don't belong there, I've spent a lot more time introducing it with a caution note. For any novice to the area, I would suggest following someone around who really knows it well; studying it very carefully from down below so you know what you're approaching on the descent; and never going up there immediately after a powder dump. As far as the specifics of what is there, it's really obvious once you take the time to study the area. Though I'm sure filmers and fellow photogs will gripe at me for talking about it at all, all I can suggest to them is that they get off their lazy asses and go glorify the "backcountry" in some other part of Tahoe so that everyone doesn't come here just to ride what the pros do.

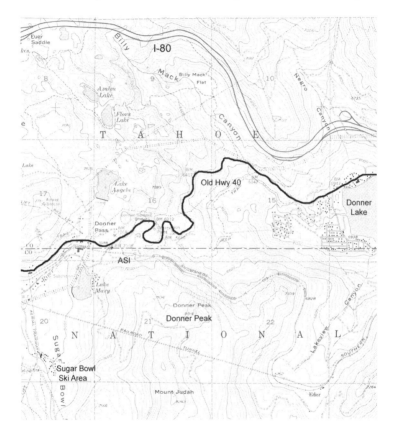

On the other side of the road, wedged between I-80 and Highway 40, is the area called Billy Mack. Most of the pitches are extremely short, though there are some surprisingly good size cliff bands tucked away in the deeper reaches of it. Depending on which side of it you want to do, you can access it from the roadside parking on Old 40 or the Billy Mack Rest Area on I-80. Even more so than ASI, this area has been a stock location for filmers over the years, due to ease of access and relative safety on deeper powder days.

Pete Brinkerhoff, Billy Mack

Donner Peak

The west face of Donner Peak (8019') is a massive bowl with some good rock drops at the top, but the really interesting side of it is the north face. This is probably some of the best exposure to be found in the Donner backcountry. It takes a solid year (15'+ base) to even become do-able, and even then it's still hairball. The area just below the summit is a collection of 45 degree pitches through a tricky 400' cliff band. Down from the summit on either side are more reasonable lines. To rider's right there are a number of challenging chutes and technical lines, and to the left there's a huge open bowl.

If you're going to bother coming over here, you might as well do a lake run. That's what Donner Peak is all about. Air over the train sheds and keep going until the snow runs out, for about 1800' of vertical. There are all kinds of rollers, staircase drops, and the like all the way down. Walk back over to Old 40 and hitch a ride back to the top of the pass.

Donner Peak

Again, this is one of the most popular easy access hikes, and the avalanche danger is considerable. There was a near fatality here in February 2001 where a snowboarder was buried, and I've watched other riders on avalanche-prone days come down these slopes with no business being on them. On a day I quit riding ASI because of loose slabs, I watched a rider come down the Donner Peak bowl and was surprised it didn't slide on him. Worse yet, while the rider watched from just above the train sheds, his barely competent buddy traversed a long path across the top of the slope. Without any clue, he was ski cutting the entire bowl, inviting it to unload on his friend below him.

Castle Peak/Basin Peak/Mt Lola

Though Castle Peak (9103') is one of the highest peaks in the Donner Region, there's only so much to be said for it as a backcountry destination. With all of the terrain on the other side of I-80, it's hard to justify doing a lot more hiking for less reward. There are some fun rock drops not too far from the road off of Andesite Peak (8219'), and the main chute off the top of Castle is an okay one. The problem with the upper part of the peak is that it's the most windblown face around and it's virtually always icy in the chute.

The way to do Castle Peak to make it more interesting is to spend a night out at Peter Grubb Hut. This is one of the backcountry huts run by the Sierra Club, and it's the most popular one. Reservations are $10/night (530-426-3632) and have to be made awhile in advance to assure that you get in. If you hike up the ridge to climber's left of Castle, the hut is down on the valley floor to the NW of the peak. The terrain off this side of Castle is kind of mellow, so you have to venture out some distance from

Kern Barta, Frog Lake Cliffs   (photo: Grant Barta)

the hut to find things worth doing. Just to the east of Castle Peak is a cliff band over Frog Lake, and this is the peak's most interesting terrain. It's steep and varied, running around a thousand feet top to bottom, and you can ride a lot of different lines here depending on the coverage.

Immediately north of Castle Peak along the Pacific Crest is Basin Peak (9015'), which has some small cliff bands on its NE side around Paradise, Warren, and Devil's Oven lakes. The shots aren't much more than two to four hundred feet of vertical, but like Frog Lake Cliffs there are a lot of different steep lines to choose from. The next peak to the north on the Crest is Mt Lola (9143'), which has a lot of nice powder turn terrain but nothing too challenging.

Jaison LeRoy

Anderson Peak

The Pacific Crest running from Mt Lincoln at Sugar Bowl back to Anderson Peak is an often-stared-at region of backcountry. Everything is steep that drops off this ridge down into Coldstream Canyon, and cornice drops are plentiful. The main consideration is access, because for most snowboarders it's just not a day trip kind of deal. Fortunately it has the best located hut out of the Sierra Club system.

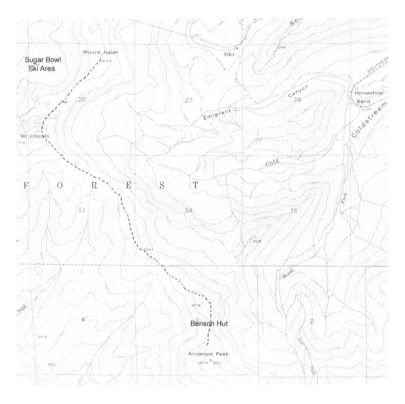

Benson Hut is located up on top of the ridge right beside Anderson Peak. Though Peter Grubb Hut needs reservations well in advance to be sure of securing it, far fewer people use Benson Hut. Still, plan in advance because more and more people are discovering the Sierra Club huts finally. The $10/night cost supports an excellent organization and a damn good hut system. Huts in Colorado are already heavily used and more expensive, so if you're going to use a hut, make sure you support and respect the people who are running the hut system. It's almost impossible to build new ones because of the bureaucracy involved with getting Forest Service permits. Treasure the ones there are.

Benson Hut   (photo: Kern Barta)

What you get is a hut usually stocked with firewood and a wood stove you can cook on, but you need to pack all your bedding and supplies in and out. All that, and the chance to walk out your door in the morning, watch a gorgeous backcountry sunrise, strap in and bomb down some great lines. The Sierra Club's hut system has only worked to date because of volunteers keeping the huts maintained, so do your part to leave it a bit better than you found it. Because this one is used less frequently, you may well have to dig out an entrance to the door if you venture to it in mid-winter.

Grant Barta, Anderson Ridge   (photo: Kern Barta)

There are a number of ways to access Benson Hut. The easiest is via Sugar Bowl, from the top of the Silver Belt Chair on Mt Lincoln. You have to check out with ski patrol and then it's a couple of miles of hiking the ridge line until you're back to Anderson Peak. Alternately you can buy a single ride ticket up the Judah chair and hike back around to Lincoln and the Anderson Ridge. Again, it's a good idea to let ski patrol know what you're doing. For the budget route, hike up from ASI all the way to the antenna shields on top of Judah and back around. (If you're *really* adventurous you can try catching on to a slow moving freight train in

Truckee and jumping off when it slows again at Horseshoe Bend, but this isn't for the faint at heart.)

The ridge has long been popular with backcountry skiers who can skate out it fairly easily, and the 500'-1000' lines have plenty of reward for their efforts. There are a lot of fantastic short steeps, but without a split board or approach skis, it's a little less worth it for a snowboarder. A spine runs off the main ridge, just north of Anderson Peak, to the northeast and down to a sub-peak at 7600'. The north face of this sub-peak has some serious steeps dropping off for a thousand feet to the valley floor. There is quite a lot of terrain like this hidden from most views, but you really need to spend a night out there to take full advantage of it.

Carson Pass/Mokelumne Wilderness

Some of the longest-lasting spring and summer backcountry is off of Carson Pass down near the Kirkwood ski resort on Highway 88. As good as it is, though, the winter backcountry is that much better and sees surprisingly few users. The king daddy of the peaks here is Round Top (10,381'), and you've got a couple more ten granders on the other side of the road with Stevens Peak and Red Lake Peak. Like Desolation, Mokelumne Wilderness is a federal wilderness area that forbids snowmobiles or any other mechanized form of travel. It extends south from Carson Pass to the Mokelumne River.

This area has been a Sierra backcountry staple for years, and one time I was up there I met an old-timer who used to ski it in the Fifties and Sixties. Back then the road wasn't open year-round. He and his buddies would park five miles below down in Hope Valley, and trek all the way to below Round Top to spend the night. There's your old school for you.

Hiking south from the Sno Park at the summit on Highway 88 (make sure you have a permit or it's a $75 fine, and the CHP does love to hand those tickets out) to Winnemucca Lake takes a bit less than an hour. The lake is a good place to use as a base camp for overnight stays, because all the chutes and bowls from Elephant's Back across to Round Top and beyond to the Sisters are more or less equidistant from it. The summit of Round Top is one of the most all-encompassing views of the Northern Sierra. It's best reached by hiking to the west side of the peak up an open face and then climbing up the ridge. To the southeast rolls the endless, jagged white of Ebbetts and Sonora passes, and to the north the deep blue of Tahoe. Just off the backside the slope drops steeply for over 2500' into a deep canyon that holds Summit City Creek.

Across the other side of Summit City Creek is Deadwood Peak (9846'), which descends through a jaw-dropping set of steeps for over two thousand feet to Blue Lakes. The down side? It's such deep access it's not even funny.

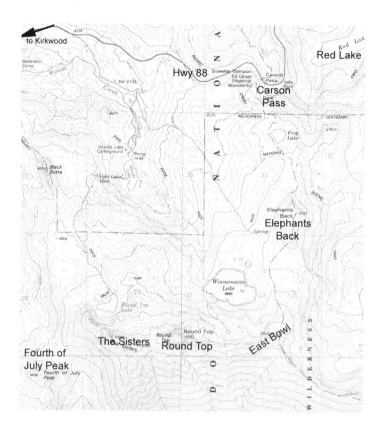

The main chute of Round Top, called Moon Crescent Chute, is one of the classics of the Northern Sierra. About 500' of vertical, it has an angled entry off the top that leaves you for a moment on top of a gigantic steep headwall before you gain the relative safety of the chute. In a macking snow year, a few insane possibilities open up on the headwall face but the consequences of screwing up are huge. I talked to a skier once who inadvertently found himself on this face staring down at 60-80' cliff drops, and he wisely got out his crampons and ice axe and climbed back to the top again. To skier's right there's another chute that joins Moon Crescent toward the bottom, which I always believed there was no top entry into. There is a short, board-width hallway into it, in fact, which I discovered when I finally did it in March 2000. Both chutes are the same relentless pitch, entry to exit, and a first class adrenaline thrill.

The trick about Moon Crescent is that it's impossible to see over the rollover at the top, so unless you're familiar with it you want to make damn sure it's actually the chute entry you're standing over. More often than not I see the exit piled up with slide rubble, too, so it's one to take extra care on regarding conditions.

Top: Moon Crescent Chute in a typical snow year   Bottom: In a huge year

Between Elephant's Back and Round Top is a string of cliff bands with more than a dozen chutes. A dramatic cliff wall runs from the east side of Round Top over to East Bowl, and there are a bunch of tight chutes tucked in these cliffs. They're all only a hundred feet long or so, but some are as thread-the-needle as you can get. In East Bowl there are a number of wide, easy chutes, with nice cornice buildups that you can air into them from. The descent around this side of the lake is fun, with plenty of steep shots down into the lake itself at the end of the run.

Dave Frissyn, East Bowl   Jason Brown

To climber's right of Round Top is a pair of peaks called The Sisters. The east peak of The Sisters (10,153') has a steep, quick shot from the top through a mini-chute and out into the bowl. The west peak (10,045') has some nice upper steeps, too, but the lines on both these peaks are so short that they're not worth seeking out on their own merit. On the other hand, if you're hiking Round Top and you need a backup plan if Moon Crescent seems questionable – which has been my experience 80% of the time - then the Sisters are your best option. Beyond The Sisters is Fourth of July Peak (9536'), which has a small, fun, back bowl visible from Round Top, and the other side edges toward the boundaries of Kirkwood.

Getting back to your car at Carson Pass from Winnemucca Lake is a bit of an art form, and requires a few trips to get it right. There's so much flat forest terrain that you can't get a good idea of where you are, and the ski tracks of the main trail diverge wildly toward the end. The safest way is to stay far to your right, just under the west face of Elephant's Back. If you veer off course, no big deal. You'll hit the road sooner or later. Though the hike in never seems that bad to me, it always seems to take forever to get back out, so save some energy for the exit.

Liz McMillan, S-carving one of the chutes above Winnemucca Lake

The east side of Elephant's Back has some sick terrain off the top of the peak, with a chute down the middle that's a mandatory air into a tight straightline. On the more sane level there are some nice short steep lines off to skier's right. Down the ridge to the north it gets mellower quickly, and there are good cornice drops to be had. Again, be wary. The cornices get heavily wind loaded. A friend of mine saw a couple of snowboarders take out a whole group below them by breaking off a cornice here. All of it drops into a wide open bowl, and if you keep following the fall line you'll come out down near the bottom of the pass at Red Lake. There's a parking area down at the south end of the lake that you can run shuttles back to the top of the pass.

Dave Frissyn, near Elephant's Back

Also out this way is another set of peaks that branches off the ridge behind East Bowl, and extends out to the east. There are some great cliff drops, chutes, and big bowl lines to be had, and they rarely get ridden. This ridge line dead ends at The Nipple out by Blue Lakes. A better way of accessing these peaks is by skiing in on the road through Hope Valley (five miles northeast of Carson Pass off of Highway 88) and camping.

East Bowl between Round Top and Elephant's Back – for reference the picture of
Dave Frissyn on p.107 is among the cliff bands in the upper left

Red Lake Peak and Stevens Peak

On the north side of the road at Carson Pass is Red Lake Peak
(10,063'), which is a more direct hike than anything on the other side, but
I've had little interesting in exploring it. The terrain isn't striking, with
long open pitches and a few rock lines. The other problem is the major
face of the peak, the south face, gets melted out a lot more quickly than the
Round Top side of the pass. In addition, the local authorities don't like you
hiking it in winter for fear of an avalanche shutting down the pass. Off the
northeast side of Red Lake Peak, there's a promising little east-facing
cirque of steeps dropping into Crater Lake.

Stevens Peak (10,059'), the next peak to the north, is a whole
different story. It has many different faces and sub-peaks, and there's a
wealth of steep terrain on it. You don't get the elevation advantage of pass
hiking, instead having to start down around 7400', but there are all kinds
of crazy chutes both off the NE face of the summit and lower down facing
Hwy 88. There's also a great south face gully descent that takes you back
down the shortest hiking route up it.

Beware of some gaping death traps on the east face of Stevens around the Alpine Mine, where open mine shafts wait to devour the unfortunate soul who steps into them. The peak is reasonably popular with Kirkwood area telemarkers, but not often done by alpine skiers and snowboarders. On the west face of Stevens, there's even more terrain to be explored. For accessing this terrain an approach from the top of Carson Pass is easier, though it's a long cross-country hike and you're riding away from the pass. The hike back over Meiss Gap to return to Highway 88 isn't bad, though, barely climbing up before dropping down to the highway at 8000' or so.

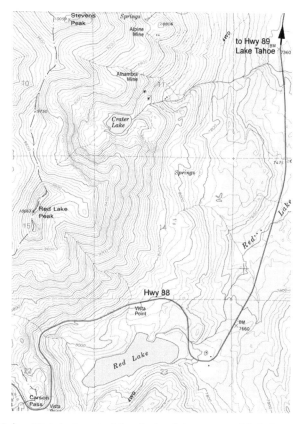

The Meiss Hut is located back in this area, which is run by David Beck and Sierra Ski Touring. It's perched up at 8500' in the uppermost reaches of the valley that holds the headwaters of the Upper Truckee River. Sandwiched between Little Round Top on one side and the north faces of Stevens Peak and Red Lake Peak on the other, it has a superb location. Unlike the Sierra Club huts, though, the Meiss Hut can only be used by arranging a guided trip through Sierra Ski Touring. The hut was built in the 1870's, making it the oldest in the Tahoe area, and it's possible the legendary Snowshoe Thompson even used it in his travels.

For Meiss Hut reservations: (775) 782-3047
http://highsierra.com/sst/ski/meiss.htm
    Sierra Ski Touring/Husky Express
    PO Box 176
    Gardnerville, NV 89410

Dave Frissyn

Echo Summit

The peaks near Echo Summit mostly fall outside the southern edges of Desolation Wilderness, though in some cases the summits are the boundary line. A mandatory stop on the way is at Chris' Cafe in Meyers, an old hangout of the South Lake Extreme Breakfast Club. (I discovered over time that the South Lake backcountry crew looked down their nose at the backcountry of the north end of the lake, and viewed themselves as that *wee* bit more hardcore. But guys like Dan Hunt won almost every extreme snowboarding championship there was in the US, and the terrain is bigger and badder at the south end, so who's to argue?) Also stop by Vertical Drop Snowboards, because the owner is a backcountry veteran and he runs a cool little shop.

Coming up Highway 50 from Meyers when you first start climbing the summit, you're confronted with an impressive ridge of steeps in front of you that stretches off to the north. Not far to your right is Flagpole Peak (8363'), which has an amazing collection of cliff lines that need a huge amount of snow to fill in properly.

North of Flagpole Peak on the ridge is Echo Peak (8895'), ringed by huge cornices on top and spotted with cliff lines down to Angora Lakes below. The cornices get very scary from severe windloading, so be extra cautious on top of them. The cliff lines above the lake are pretty tricky, with only a handful of lines through them. Definitely scope before you drop.

Winter access to the Flagpole-Echo ridge is something of a bitch, which is why it gets done rarely. Some people hike it all the way from the Sno Park at Echo Summit, and others slog in from the front side. No route is easy. Because of avalanche danger to the road, everything right above Highway 50 on the way to the summit is off limits during winter, which rules out the most direct access. When you're planning a route, figure in an extra few hours because you'll likely need them. Both my hikes out here in '99 ended with people struggling the last mile, sorely fatigued and cursing me roundly.

Directly to the south of Echo Peak, on the other side of Upper and Lower Echo Lake, are Talking Mountain (8824') and Becker Peak (8321').

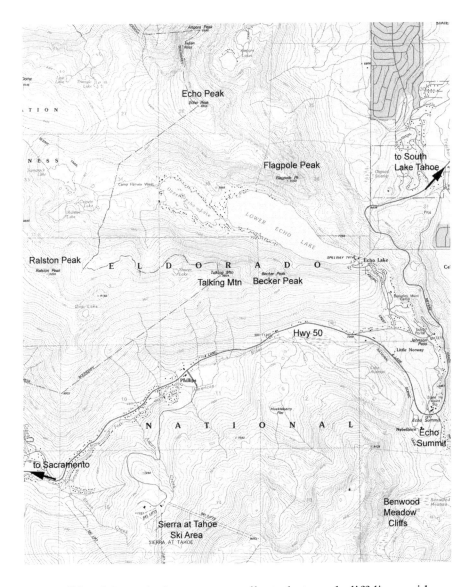

Talking Mountain has some excellent chute and cliff lines midway down its north face, and a great variety of steep 1200-1400' runs down to the frozen lakes below. Becker has shorter runs, but some nice tree chute lines.

To the west is Ralston Peak (9235'), which has a line of fun cornices above a steep open face on the ridge to the southwest of it. Off the peak down to Ralston Lake, the first thousand feet is a very steep descent with some dramatic cliff sections to thread your way through or go as big as you could possibly want off of. An easier descent to skier's left, north on the ridge, takes you down through an open face of giant rollers down to the lake. The descent from peak to lake is a solid 2400', a serious leg burn.

Top: Echo Peak   Bottom: Talking Mountain, seen from Echo Peak

The descents of these peaks on the south side to Highway 50 is less interesting, though there's a lake near the top of the ridge on the south face near Ralston called Cup Lake, and just near it there are some cliff lines. Still, the vertical is substantial and it's a nice long descent to go out on. Access to Talking Mountain and Becker Peak is best gained from the Echo Lakes Sno Park on the north side of the summit, for which you must buy a $5 day pass or $20 seasonal permit (December-April). Ralston Peak is so far west that it makes sense to park lower down on Highway 50 and hike straight up via Cup Lake, because it only adds on an additional 400 feet of vertical to the hike.

Ralston Peak

The truly blessed among the South Lake backcountry crew are those whose families have passed down through the generations one of the backcountry cabins scattered around the Echo Lakes or Angora Lakes. For the rest of us, there is still an option for securing convenient and cheap lodging at the top of the pass. The California Alpine Club runs the Echo Summit Lodge, where beds are available to members for only $20 a night or so. To join the club, you need to attend a meeting, get an understanding of their philosophy, and find an existing member who will sponsor you. Information is available on their website, www.calpine.org, or by phone at

415-457-9028. The club is based out of Mill Valley in the Bay Area, and is committed to "leave no trace" alpine activities.

Across Highway 50 on the south side of the summit, the Pacific Crest drops off steeply into the Christmas Valley. Some of this terrain is a stone's throw from the backside of Sierra-at-Tahoe resort, and relatively accessible from the Benwood Meadow parking area just off the summit. There's still a fair bit of vertical hiking involved, though, as most of the steeps begin 1000' above the meadow. Following the Crest further south, there are a number of dramatic sections of cliff band steeps falling to the valley floor.

the author, Echo Peak   (photo: Dave Frissyn)

Ebbetts Pass

Ebbetts Pass is one of the best kept secrets in the Sierra, and has become my favorite mountain pass in the whole range. It may not have one concentrated section quite as dramatic as Third Pillar at Tioga Pass, nor the sheer depth of terrain of Sonora Pass, but in its totality I'll put it up against any of them. Nowhere else has as many continuous 2000-3000' descent lines, nor as many challenging short steeps. Besides its outstanding terrain, I think the main charm of Ebbetts is that it's so damn remote and inaccessible. Thus I don't mind singing its praises, because it falls into the realm for 99.9% of the public of "places you'd love to go but never will". It's one of the last passes in the Sierra to open because it's the least used of them. By the time Cal Trans plows it all the way through - at earliest mid-May and sometimes as late as mid-June - the snow is melted back so badly that a lot of the best lines aren't possible and/or the snow is fairly rotten. And if you snowmobilers are sitting there smugly saying "I can get the goods", be warned that the east side road is closed all the way back to the Monitor Pass turnoff in winter yet still dry for five miles most of the time. If you want to drive all the way around to the Bear Valley side

Erik Wilhelm, Pass Ridge

Dave Frissyn scouting past the gate

and sled sixteen miles up to the pass, be my guest. Ebbetts protects itself
well from incursion.

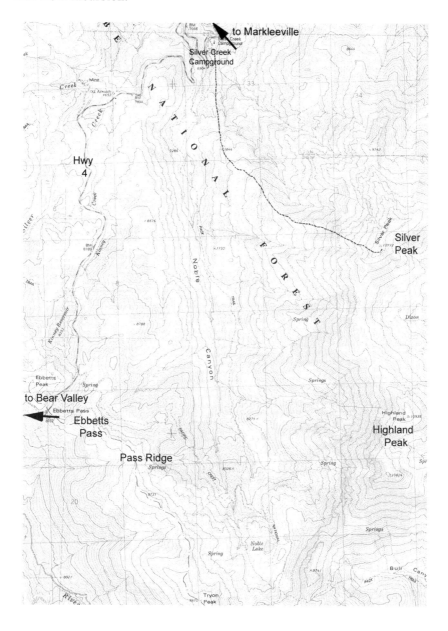

Silver Peak (10,772' on the south peak, 10,800' on the north peak) is the first peak you encounter coming in from the east. The NE face has a large upper bowl with a couple of chutes in the dominant cliff band, before the slopes roll away gently toward the Carson River. One of the chutes looks very promising from a distance, about 300' long and steep as hell. On the NW face of the mountain, a huge gash splits the rock for 1200', which Dave Frissyn first noticed from twenty-five miles away. We had been in Desolation, hiking to Halls of the Gods for the first time, when Dave wondered what the enormous chute in the distance was.

Because Halls of the Gods had not quite lived up to its billing in terms of size, we were still on the lookout for a genuine thousand footer in the Northern Sierra. That image we saw from Echo Peak burned deep into our minds, and we consulted our topo's until we confirmed it was Silver Peak down at Ebbetts we were looking at. On a spring day before the road was open, we drove down with our mountain bikes and rode up from the gate at Silver Creek Campground. After a few false starts, we climbed to a good vantage point and watched the midday sun creep its way into the chute. It was a beautiful thing to behold, a chute of that size whose existence I'd never heard anyone mention.

Dave and I sat on a ridge a couple of miles away and shook our heads in awe. It wasn't nearly as steep as the other classic chutes, but boy were the walls of it big. After one memorable late season powder day in early May, we saw a window to do it and charged down there again.

Though I thought our five hour climb was lengthened by route-finding, difficulty finding a creek crossing, and general pokiness, Grant Barta told me he took the exact same amount of time when he did it a couple of weeks later. Once up near the top, the views from where we were of the rest of Ebbetts Pass confirmed our suspicions about just how much epic backcountry surrounded Noble Canyon. A lifetime of lines.

Since we didn't know a name for the main chute off of Silver, we decided to call it Glider Chute. It was way the hell up there and it was so wide open and fast that you swooped your way down it. Despite their remoteness, the chutes of the Southern Sierra are all well documented historically as far as first descents, and have established names. Some of the biggest chutes of the Northern Sierra, while more accessible, have no names I've ever heard anyone agree upon and are so rarely done that finding out any history of descents is well nigh impossible.

Silver Peak

I have no illusions that there are any first ski descents left in the Northern Sierra, though I wouldn't be surprised if Dave's descent of Glider Chute was the first snowboard descent. I realized its obscurity was due to it being hidden from view from most angles. You only see half of it from anywhere on the road at Ebbetts. If it hadn't been for Dave's wandering eye that day on Echo Peak, it might have been a long time before we ever became aware of it.

Glider Chute is only the beginning of the descent, and below it is another good 2500' of assorted gully lines, mini-chutes, and cliff drops all the way back to Silver Creek. Following the ascent ridge back to the creek takes you through some very fun terrain, and is a better guarantee of a successful exit, but the sub-peak below the exit of Glider Chute is a launching point for another great descent. You have to climb a few hundred feet up the peak, but then you're staring straight down a beautiful chute that empties into a long gully run with endless walls to surf.

Further up the pass on your right is Raymond Peak (10,014'), which is set back a few miles from the road and doesn't have much to look at on its south face beyond a few small chute lines. The descent toward the road crosses a couple of valleys and isn't worth the hike. The most interesting thing about the terrain around this part of Raymond are the jagged spires which leap out everywhere. Silver has some of them too, and they seem much more characteristic of the Southern Sierra than anywhere in the Tahoe region. I suspect that Ebbetts melts out faster than Carson Pass because there's so much more of this sort of exposed rock that heats up.

Erik Wilhelm

Off the north side of Raymond are a number of different steep, rock-laden faces. The vertical drop off this side is better, running about 1500-2000' before bottoming out on the valley floor a few miles from Blue Lakes. Doing this terrain is only practical during a Carson-Ebbetts crest tour. It's actually one of the easier pass-to-pass tours, since much of it is along the floor of the Hope Valley, along the snow-covered road that runs from Highway 88 some seven miles back to Blue Lakes.

As you approach the top of the pass, Highland Peak (10,935' north peak, 10,824' south peak) looms up directly to the south of Silver Peak. There are at least a half dozen beautiful descents off its north face, 2000' gullies with at least one solid chute in each one. One of the lines off the west ridge has a thread-the-needle chute about six feet wide and a hundred feet long.

south summit of Highland Peak in early June - imagine the lines in winter

Just off the top of the pass on the north side is Ebbetts Peak (9600'), which has some interesting, quick steeps on its east face. You can ride off this face across a plateau and down another steep 400' face of trees and rocks into Kinney Reservoir. A few miles before the top of the pass on the same side of the road is a similar face dropping into a lake.

Off the top of the pass on the south side is an innocent looking dome no more than 300' of vertical climbing from the road, but once you're on it you look down its east face at a beautiful set of *steep* 300-500' chute and tech lines. This ridge extends southeast toward Highland Peak, forming the top end of Noble Canyon. The farther you go out, the crazier the terrain gets. What I thought was amazing the first two times I went there turned out to be an insignificant blip compared to the outlying terrain on this ridge.

outer limits of Pass Ridge

These spots are the highlights of Ebbetts Pass, but there's more in the area, particularly during full winter coverage. If you have the gumption to make it up there before the snow melts, there's a seemingly endless paradise of some of the finest boarding and skiing in the Northern Sierra, and you're unlikely to run into anyone else. What's interesting about Ebbetts Pass being the most "forgotten" pass of the Sierra Nevada is that it was the first pass to ever be crossed in the range, when the legendary mountain man and trader Jedediah Smith used it as a route in 1827. This was more than twenty years before the Donner Party made its disastrous attempt to the north of Lake Tahoe.

Sonora Pass

After my first trip to Sonora Pass in 1995, I thought it was a fun place with some nice runs close to the top of the pass, but the good terrain was impossibly far back. Even then, I wasn't sure how much truly classic terrain there was. An assignment for the now-defunct *Snowboard Life* in 2000 turned my ideas about the pass upside down. I had the fortune to hook up with pro snowboarder Adam Hostetter and his traveling palace, a 42' RV towing a truck with two snowmobiles in the back. It was one of the only times I've ever done backcountry by snowmobile, but it helped me discover far more terrain at Sonora Pass than I ever knew existed.

Erik Wilhelm   Nate Holland

There are three gates on the road up the pass, and the first one is out by Highway 395, and closed most of the winter. The second one is just past the Mountain Warfare Training Center - the base for America's most elite mountain troops, the descendants of the legendary 10th Mountain

Division - and this gate is often closed into April. The final one is at 7155', just before the road begins to radically climb, and usually doesn't open until late May or June.

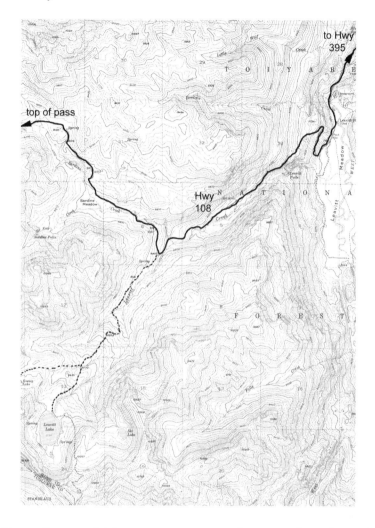

Depending on which gates are open, you have to trek up the road until you hit the snow line and then strap on your approach skis. Though this adds to an already long approach, in springtime it does have the benefit of limiting snowmobilers who don't want to run their sleds over pavement to the snow line.

There is another option, if the snow levels have been reasonably low and the weather has stayed cold, and you don't want to make the long approach up the pass. Instead of climbing the pass road, start out between the second and final gate at Leavitt Meadow and follow the West Walker River south through the valley. Because this is the far east side of the range, it's not likely to have good coverage to the valley floor most of the time. If it does, though, there are two thousand foot descents on either side of the valley that rank with many of the ones deeper in the mountains. The valley is also a beautiful place for winter camping, and fairly well protected.

In the April trip that I did, we started from the snowline just past the final gate (a key fairy got us past it). In winter and early spring conditions the best approach is to ski up the road from the gate about 3.5 miles until you reach the turnoff to Leavitt Lake. When there is little trace of the road and the signs are buried under snow, you will recognize this turnoff by the fact that the bulk of the ski and sled tracks have gone in this direction (southwest). The main road takes a hard turn back to the north right here, so when following the turnoff it actually appears that you're staying on the main road. It's a gentle ascent for a little less than three miles up this valley to Leavitt Lake, climbing from 8400' to 9556'.

Leavitt Lake

At the lake, you find yourself at the base of a breathtaking cirque, surrounded by a series of nearly eleven thousand foot peaks. There are nasty steeps lines to be had in this cirque, but they do melt out fairly quickly in spring. For better snow coverage, backtrack a quarter mile and climb west over the ridge, up the drainage to Koenig Lake (9588'). A 10,870' peak with a huge, steep east face looms above Koenig, dotted with a variety of chutes. Above the southeast end of the lake is a beautiful diagonal chute coming off of a 10,400' peak. Along the ridge dividing Koenig from Leavitt Lake, there are myriad possibilities for jumps and cornice drops. To the northwest from Koenig there is a fun gully that leads down from Latopie Lake (10,389'), with great walls to surf and slash.

Adam Hostetter, below Latopie Lake

If you were to climb up to the saddle just above Latopie, you would find yourself on the Pacific Crest, and looking down the north face of another good cirque. This is about three miles dead south of the top of Sonora Pass, and the mighty Leavitt Peak (11,569') is only a short hike up the ridge to the southwest.

Leavitt Peak

For a multi-day camping tour, you could follow the crest north back to the main road at the top of the pass, and ski down the road back to your car. Since this is getting mighty far afield from where you started, I will look at Leavitt Peak and its cirque from the point of view of starting a trip from the top of the pass. This is how I did it on my first trip, in early summer.

Looking south from the parking area at the summit, you see a peak (11,040') that has some rock at the top and a very short central chute, dropping into a large open bowl. Following the crest ridge from the road will get you there in less than an hour. Look to your climber's right as you climb the ridge and on the west side of the crest you'll see a big cornice that drops into another bowl. This descends through a great gully run out to the road, a mile or so down the west side of the pass. Above the cornice is a plateau that gives you a panoramic view of Leavitt Peak and the Deadman and Blue Canyon cirques two to three miles farther back. The Pacific Crest keeps meandering south of Leavitt Peak into the areas already described, but an even higher spine breaks off to the west and curves back north toward toward the road.

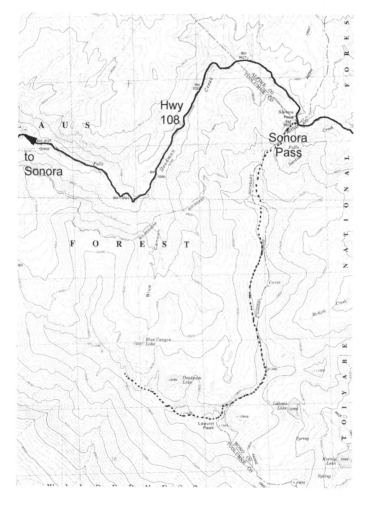

This ridge above Deadman Lake and Blue Canyon Lake is punctuated by peaks of 11,470' and a couple above 11,200'. Some epic chutes drop from these peaks into the valley below. The runs off this ridge are mostly about 1000' of vertical or less, so you can hike back up and knock off a number of lines as you head north back to the road.

Deadman Chute

The exit run from the valley takes you from Blue Canyon Lake down Blue Canyon to the road, about 2.7 miles west of the summit. The run is very flat at first, and then begins to descend more rapidly. When it first starts to drop away, traverse over to skier's left and hike up to the top of the ridge. This puts you above an amazing 1200' face of steeps that comes out right at the road. These lines are not for the faint of heart, though, and you might want to stick to the canyon run if you're not up for one last giant adrenaline thrill.

The Nooks and Crannies

There are places all throughout the Northern Sierra well away from Lake Tahoe and the mountain passes that are host to great terrain. These spots are off the radar of most lake-based backcountry enthusiasts. Some of them are far from hidden, like the mountains on either side of I-80 that greet travelers coming up to Tahoe from Sacramento and the Bay Area. These peaks whet the appetite of most people, but are thought of as no more than a preface to the larger peaks to come. Much more off the beaten path are places like the Sierra Buttes, well known as a summer hiking and mountain biking area but less known for the staggering winter steeps it has to offer.

Because I have only scouted these places, and not ridden them, most of my knowledge is from second-hand reports and recognition of their potential.

author scouting in summer for winter lines   (photo: Royce Burton)

Sierra Buttes

The Sierra Buttes have long been popular as a destination for spring telemarkers, but are increasingly seeing winter traffic as more skiers and snowboarders discover snowmobiles. Located off of Highway 49 some eight miles west of Yuba Pass, the Buttes are most famous for being the starting point of California's most epic mountain bike downhill. Running eighteen miles from the Buttes to Downieville, the Downieville Downhill descends from 7000' to 2800' elevation. Some fifty miles to the north of the bustle of Tahoe, this whole region hasn't seen much action since the gold rush days. It's the only place where I've downhill skated a mountain pass road in summer that a CHP officer has been more interested if I'd seen cows in the road causing a hazard than caring about me being one.

Ben Bleichman, Sierra Buttes   (photo: Grant Barta)

A road forks off of Highway 20 at Bassetts, where there's a general store and restaurant, and leads back to the Buttes. The road is closed in winter, though, making the approach so long that only snowmobilers use this area much. The problem for them, often, is whether there is enough snow at Bassetts, which is only about 5400' elevation.

The approach in spring is from the resort at Lower Sardine Lake, following the forest road up to Upper Sardine Lake, and hugging the west edge of it up to the foot of the Buttes. From there you have an infinity of choices. The Buttes contain a wild array of steeps lines and cliff drops packed into a highly concentrated area. Huge, jagged cliffs divide up the faces, so that each further adventure around a corner reveals a whole new wonderland.

There is some debate about whether the Sierra Buttes are even part of the Sierra Nevada, or whether they are a tiny mountain range of their own. Certainly they form the most northern boundary of any notable mountains that are part of the Sierra. The next large peaks to the north are the volcanic ones of Lassen National Park. The top of the Sierra Buttes only peaks out at 8591', and most of the terrain is at 8000' or less, with a maximum vertical descent of about two thousand feet to Upper Sardine Lake.

west face of the Sierra Buttes, above Young American Lake

East on I-80

Cisco Butte

I never particularly noticed this small butte (6639') on the south side of the Cisco Grove exit of I-80 in all my drives up and down the highway, but I was impressed by the helmet cam video that Dave Frissyn supplied me from a trip with his brother. It's a ridiculously easy hike, only some 800' of vertical, but the main chute off the peak is a beauty. All you have to do is park, cross the railroad tracks and climb straight up it toward the relay towers.

Old Man Mountain

This rarely skied mountain sits six miles north of I-80 and some ten miles west from Donner Summit. Because it's one of the westernmost peaks in the range of any note, and lower elevation than most, it doesn't get done a whole lot. The access problem is a big part of it. Most people wouldn't consider it worth the effort when there are so many other bigger mountains that are more accessible. There's some incredible terrain on it for the adventurous, though.

The SW face of Old Man Mountain (7789') is the steepest part, with some forty five degree chutes that are best with a moderate base before the face fills in too much. You get a good view of them from around the Highway 20 exit on I-80. Off the summit down the south face is mostly open carving, but there are a few challenging rock lines on it, and it's a good 1800' fast run down to Fordyce Creek. Around the corner on the east face are some nice cliff bands, and though the runs are much shorter there's great hucking potential in this part.

A trip to Old Man Mountain is best started from the Eagle Lakes exit, at the entrance to the National Forest road to Fordyce Pass. You can spend a long time traversing around the base of Signal Peak or you can save time by taking a direct approach and climbing straight up Signal Peak and then skiing off the north face to the base of Old Man Mountain. This makes for a good trip if you camp along Fordyce Creek in the valley between the two mountains. Without a split board or skis, though, don't think about it.

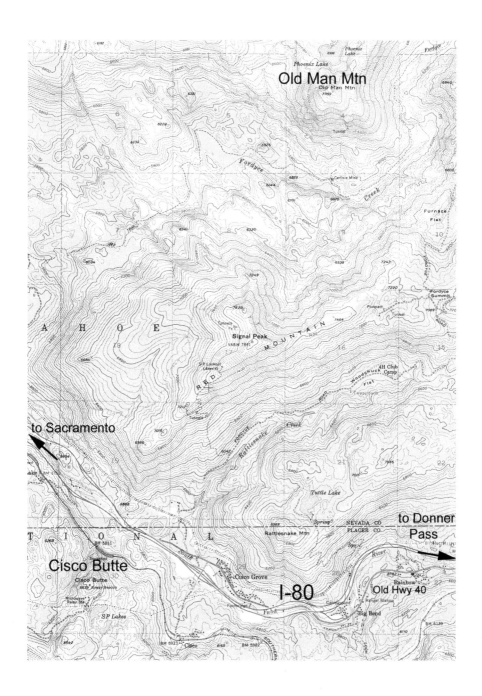

Hawkins Peak

A gem on the eastern side of the range that most people pay no attention, just south of Highway 88, is Hawkins Peak (10,024'). As you come down Luther Pass on the way south, it appears to be as pointless a ten grander as Freel Peak. The summit area is a broad, flat plateau. Because most people turn right on Highway 88 to head up to Carson Pass and Kirkwood, they never see the amazing steeps this mountain has to offer. If you turn left on to Highway 89 toward Markleeville, you'll soon catch a glimpse.

Cloudburst Canyon, which funnels into Highway 89 a few miles east of Sorensens store, comes off the plateau and divides a set of cliffs with a staggering array of steep chute lines. Because Carson Pass intercepts the vast bulk of snow of storms moving across this region, the coverage is often thin on these cliffs. In addition, there is so much exposed rock that it melts out easily. On a good snow year, though, there is a smorgasbord to sample. The steeps begin at 9400' and don't relent until just before the highway at 6000'.

Access is best from Deep Canyon, which is about 2 miles east of Sorensens. There's a parking turnoff on the north side of the road. As you climb, curve up to the left when the gully forks and you'll eventually reach the top of Hawkins Peak.

The other great face of Hawkins is the south side leading down to Grover Hot Springs. This is another tremendous cliff band full of chutes, beginning at 8600' and ending at 6000' on the valley floor, right at the hot springs. The hot springs are open year round and there's a winter camping area, so it's a fantastic place to finish off a descent. If you just want to do this face, it's probably easiest just to drive back to the hot springs and climb right up it. Depending on your equipment and whether you want a bit of a tour, though, it's a gentler ascent of Hawkins Peak from the north side, and you can do it as a shuttle trip. Grover Hot Springs State Park is reached from a turnoff in Markleeville on Highway 89, and the road winds four miles up the valley to the springs.

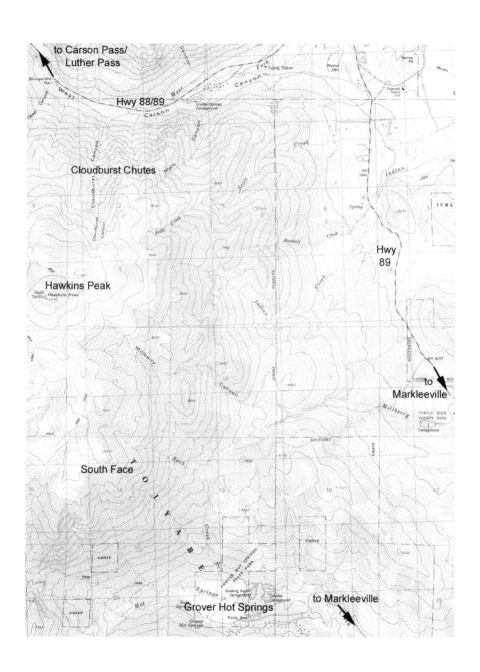

to Carson Pass/
Luther Pass

Hwy 88/89

Cloudburst Chutes

Hawkins Peak

South Face

Hwy
89

to
Markleeville

Grover Hot Springs

to Markleeville

About the Author

George Hurchalla first found himself in Tahoe in 1991, after a surf trip around the world only got as far as Australia before money ran out and he turned around. Relegated to sleeping on the floor of a tourist clothing store in Hawaii, he quickly tired of waking up under racks of muu-muus. Buying the cheapest ticket to the mainland he could, he landed in San Francisco. Four months later he moved to Tahoe. After a few weeks of experience as a rental tech at Homewood Ski Resort, he was laid off and promptly landed a prized job as a rental tech at Dave's Ski Shop in Tahoe City. Snowboarders were still an oppressed minority in Tahoe, and ones that could meet Dave's strict standards of employment – show up for work - were few and far between. Soon Hurchalla was tuning snowboards, dispensing advice, and generally acting like an old hand, despite having seen mountain snow only once before that winter.

Born and raised in south Florida, Hurchalla obtained a bachelor's degree in Mechanical Engineering from Swarthmore College in 1988. Following a career in engineering appeared to clash with his goals of traveling the world and writing, so he chose a life of insecure poverty instead and pursued his dreams. Hailing from a state whose highest elevation a good quarterback could throw a pass over, he thinks his mountain blood comes from his paternal ancestors, Slovakian peasants who lived at the foot of the High Tatras.

In 1994 Hurchalla edited the book *The Hell With Politics: The Life and Writings of Jane Wood Reno*. Buoyed by a large paycheck from an El Salvador surf photo that Rip Curl bought in 1996, Hurchalla seized the opportunity to get into a field even less lucrative than writing, and began a career as a snowboard photographer. He wrote his first snowboarding article for *Heckler Magazine* in 1997, and his first backcountry article – on Sonora Pass – in 1998. During the next few years, his photos sporadically made their way into the pages of *Transworld Snowboarding*, *Couloir*, and *Snowboard Life*. After two years of deprivation in a dank Squaw Valley basement chipped away at the illusion he was living his dreams, he took a sabbatical from snowboarding in 2001.

Returning to the surf, he wrote and photographed two Falcon Guides, *Exploring Florida's Atlantic Coast Beaches* and *Exploring Florida's Gulf*

Coast Beaches, published in November 2002. At the same time he began shooting digital video to document downhill and pool skateboarding. An avid downhill skater, Hurchalla has been working with backcountry partner Dave Frissyn to push the limits of high speed stand-up skating on Sierra mountain passes. Utilizing custom built wingsuits inspired by skydivers, they solved the problem of how to brake for hairpin curves. Routinely riding at speeds of 40-50 mph, the results of their efforts can be seen in the movie *GRIP*, being put out by Spot X Films in 2004.

cruising the lower road at Ebbetts Pass after a day of snowboarding   (photo: Dave Frissyn)